# EXPERIENCING THE PRESENCE OF GOD

# A.W. TOZER

*Compiled and Edited by* James L. Snyder

# EXPERIENCING THE
# PRESENCE OF
# GOD

## TEACHINGS FROM THE BOOK OF HEBREWS

BETHANYHOUSE
a division of Baker Publishing Group
Minneapolis, Minnesota

© 2010 by James L. Snyder

Published by Bethany House Publishers
11400 Hampshire Avenue South
Bloomington, Minnesota 55438
www.bethanyhouse.com

Bethany House Publishers is a division of
Baker Publishing Group, Grand Rapids, Michigan

Bethany House edition published 2014
ISBN 978-0-7642-1618-3

Previously published by Regal Books

Printed in the United States of America

The Library of Congress has cataloged the original edition as follows:
    Tozer, A. W. (Aiden Wilson), 1897-1963.
    Experiencing the presence of God : teachings from the book of Hebrews /
A. W. Tozer; edited by James L. Snyder.
    p. cm.
    ISBN 978-0-8307-4693-4 (trade paper)
    1. Bible. N.T. Hebrews—Sermons. 2. Christian and Missionary Alliance—Sermons. 3. Sermons, American—20th century. I. Snyder, James L. II. Title.
BS2775.54.T69  2010
227'.8706—dc22                                        2010023019

All Scripture quotations are taken from the King James Version of the Bible.

14  15  16  17  18  19  20        7  6  5  4  3  2  1

# CONTENTS

# FOREWORD

As a teenager and a brand-new Christian, one of my earliest and greatest discoveries was A. W. Tozer. From *The Knowledge of the Holy*—still my favorite nonfiction book besides the Bible—to *The Pursuit of God* and *Born After Midnight* and his other books compiled from the editorials he wrote for *The Alliance Witness* magazine, I devoured everything Tozer wrote.

I still go back to those dog-eared pages and marvel at how Christ-centered, God-exalting and no-nonsense Tozer's words remain. What do I mean by no-nonsense? Well, reading some of today's Christian writers, I've been tempted to feel pretty good about myself. But reading Tozer is like asking for a much-needed slap in the face! There should be a sticker on the cover warning readers that they will be pierced by God's Spirit. And isn't that exactly what we need in our noisy, thrill-a-minute, whatever-feels-good-is-okay culture?

Tozer was not only a great thinker and Christ-lover but also a great writer who honed his literary skills as an editor and writer of editorials. His eclectic knowledge is remarkable, and yet his style is concise and pointed. His words flow from a higher source, out of his immersion in God's Word and his own commitment to worshiping God in everything. The result is a power that can at times leave the reader breathless, yet longing for more.

I am convinced that the evangelical Church in the Western world needs A. W. Tozer more than ever. That's why I am so grateful for this previously unpublished work *Experiencing the*

*Presence of God*. What a pleasure to hear from Tozer on a subject of keen interest: God's manifest presence in the life of His people. It is a much-needed wake-up call for anyone who wants to truly worship God. It left me enriched and challenged.

Tozer is to me a mentor and an old friend. His timelessness and impact on my life is comparable to that of Charles Haddon Spurgeon. Neither man has lost an ounce of his original power and anointing, which was so firmly grounded in God's Word and the ministry of His Holy Spirit in their lives.

Tozer's words feed my mind and heart, consistently pointing me toward Christ. By rubbing shoulders with him on the pages of his books, I am led to worship God and am drawn closer to my Savior and King. There is simply no higher compliment I could pay an author.

I thank God for A. W. Tozer, and I look forward to sitting next to him at a banquet on the New Earth, where we will hear directly from our Redeemer. My advice until then is simple: read this book and read everything by A. W. Tozer you can get your hands on. In doing so, you will draw closer to Christ and invest in the eternity that awaits us.

Randy Alcorn
Bestselling author of *Heaven,*
*The Treasure Principle* and *Safely Home*
Director, Eternal Perspective Ministries

# A Journey of Discovering God's Presence

Throughout the history of humanity, there have been many great discoveries. I am not sure which one we could point to and say, "That is the greatest discovery in the world." But for the hungry heart, there is but one discovery that satisfies it: the discovery of the manifest, conscious presence of God.

This book you hold is an unveiling of Dr. Tozer's greatest discovery: to understand what God's presence in the Christian's life is all about and to experience it. Dr. Tozer is a qualified guide in this pilgrimage.

There are several things you will notice as you go through this book. First, everything that Dr. Tozer writes about is based upon solid, scriptural truth. The major point he makes is that one truth is not isolated from another truth. Isolating God's truth, according to Tozer, is how heresy starts in the Church.

When people begin isolating Scripture to try to make it stand on its own, it is a warning signal that truth will be sacrificed. It is possible to make the Bible say anything you really want it to say. After all, the cults in the world begin with the Bible, and what they do is isolate truth, failing to recognize the harmony of the truth in God's Word. Often, Dr. Tozer will say something to the effect that it takes all of the Bible to make it the Word of God.

So the scriptural foundation is very important. Many people have taken a sharp left turn somewhere and gone into what Dr. Tozer calls a Christless mysticism. Nothing could be more dangerous than this, which has led to a strange caricature of Christianity in our day.

I think the next thing you should look for in this book is what Dr. Tozer describes as the conscious, manifest presence of God. Many people decry the word "experience." However, unless you have experienced salvation, you have not been born again. And so the plea in this book is for each of us to press on and press in and experience the presence of God.

Are there charlatans along this line? Of course. But we cannot allow some heretic to rob us of truths associated with the Christian life. This basic truth before us is that it is possible for us to know God in a degree of intimacy that is progressive as well as dynamic. The apostle Paul said, "That I may know him, and the power of his resurrection, and the fellowship of his sufferings, being made conformable unto his death" (Phil. 3:10). That is the goal and what we are after: to know God in an increasing level of intimacy from day to day.

This book will whet your appetite for some of the deep things of God. I think if Dr. Tozer were alive today, he might be shocked at some of the teaching we hear over the airwaves, especially on television. The deep truths of God's Word are not being expounded in our day on any large scale.

That leads to another theme in this book. Tozer never goes easy on what he refers to as religiosity, or, as the Scripture says, "Having a form of godliness, but denying the power thereof: from such turn away" (2 Tim. 3:5). One of the things he attacks most viciously is entertainment in the Church. If you are the sort of person who craves entertainment, you may not like what you read. This message is for those who really want to know God in a way that is out of the ordinary.

A word of caution here: You might not always agree with Dr. Tozer. In fact, he would not want you to agree with him on everything. His purpose is not to win you over to his side. We have a tendency in our society to divide ourselves into little religious pigeonholes. Every little pigeonhole has to agree with everybody on everything in that particular group. If you do not agree with everything, then you must go to another pigeonhole.

Tozer thought this idea ludicrous. There are certain fundamentals of the faith to which we all must embrace and adhere, but then, as Tozer would muse, we must always allow room for mystery. So many things in the spiritual realm remain a mystery. Where we get into trouble is trying to define and describe all of the mysteries. Many of us have a Sherlock Holmes complex when it comes to spiritual things. We want to know everything to the smallest detail. This is nothing more or less than religious minutia, and it only feeds Pharisaic pride.

Striving after God and aspiring to know Him are welcome traits. But in all of this, no matter how far we go in our spiritual walk, there will still be mysteries. What Dr. Tozer teaches in this book is how to walk in the mystery of experiencing God's presence.

Included at the end of each chapter is a carefully chosen hymn or piece of poetry that sums up the truth in that chapter. It would be well worth the effort to spend some time meditating on that hymn or poem. Dr. Tozer's practice in his daily walk with the Lord was to spend time in the hymnbook. I know the hymnbook has gone out of style in many churches today, but we cannot afford to miss the rare treasure of some of these old hymns of the church!

Dr. Tozer was not one to continually look back and pine for the "good old days." But neither was he dismissive of the great history of our Christian faith. And nowhere is that history appreciated more than in the words of a good old-fashioned hymnbook. Perhaps his love of hymnody will whet your appetite to explore this rich store of doctrinal truth.

May God enable you in your spiritual journey to experience everything He has for you to experience. And may you come away from this book ready to live in the manifest, conscious presence of almighty God.

James L. Snyder

# TEACHINGS FROM THE
# BOOK OF HEBREWS

# 1

# STRIVING TOWARD GOD'S PRESENCE

*God, who at sundry times and in divers manners spake*
*in time past unto the fathers by the prophets, hath in these last days*
*spoken unto us by his Son, whom he hath appointed heir of all things,*
*by whom also he made the worlds; who being the brightness of his glory,*
*and the express image of his person, and upholding all things by the*
*word of his power, when he had by himself purged our sins,*
*sat down on the right hand of the Majesty on high.*

HEBREWS 1:1-3

In the deep recesses of man's soul lies an overwhelming yearning toward the Creator. This is a common thread through all humanity, created in the image of God. Unless and until that desire is fully met, the human soul remains restless, constantly striving for that which is ultimately unattainable.

To any discerning Christian, it is easy to see that men and women are in an awful spiritual and moral mess today. A person must know where he is before he can comprehend where he needs to be. The solution, however, is not within the scope of human endeavor. The highest ideal or accomplishment of man is to break from the spiritual bondage and enter into the presence of God, knowing that you have entered welcomed territory.

Within every human breast rages this desire, driving him forward. Many a person confuses the object of that desire and spends his or her entire life striving for the unobtainable. Very simply put, the great passion in the heart of every human being, who are created in the image of God, is to experience the awesome majesty of God's presence. The highest accomplishment of humanity is entering the overwhelming presence of God. Nothing else can satiate this burning thirst.

The average person, unable to understand this passion for intimacy with God, fills his life with things, hoping somehow to satisfy his inward longing. He chases that which is exterior, hoping to satisfy that inner thirst, but to no avail.

St. Augustine, the Bishop of Hippo, captured the essence of this desire in his *Confessions*: "Thou hast created us for Thyself and we are restless until we rest fully in Thee." This explains, to a great degree, the spirit of restlessness pervading every generation and every culture—always striving but never coming to the knowledge of the truth of God's presence.

John the Revelator voices something quite similar: "Thou art worthy, O Lord, to receive glory and honour and power: for thou hast created all things, and for thy pleasure they are and were created" (Rev. 4:11). It is God's great pleasure for us to fully rest in His presence, moment by moment. God created man expressly for the use of His pleasure and fellowship. Nothing in or of this world measures up to the simple pleasure of experiencing the presence of God.

The spirit of restlessness breaking across the sea of humanity testifies to this truth. Our whole purpose as created beings is to utilize our time delighting in the manifest presence of our

Creator. This presence is both intangible and indescribable. Some try explaining it, but only those with a personal, intimate knowledge of God's presence can truly understand. Some things rise above explanation and human understanding, and this is one. Many Christians are filled with good information, but only a few mercy drops fall into their languid soul to satisfy the thirst for God's presence. Too many have never burst into the dazzling sunlight of God's conscious, manifest presence. Or if they perchance have, it is a rare experience and not a continuous delight.

## Man's Striving for Altitude

Intimacy with the Creator separates man from all other of God's creation. The great passion buried in the breast of every human being created in the image of God is to experience this awesome majesty of His presence. However, several things stand in the way of man's striving toward the presence of God in personal, intimate familiarity.

The experience of too many people trying to probe the presence of God ends in complete and utter frustration. Longing to be in His presence and actually coming into His presence are two entirely different things. As created beings, man longs for the presence of the Creator, but in himself cannot find it.

Consider the eagle, born to fly. A natural-yearning within the breast of the young eagle leads it to mount up on wings and ascend into the sky with a thousand feet of clean air beneath its wings. The eagle may, on occasion, walk on the ground or perch in a tree, but everything about him is designed to fly in the air. If our eagle had its wings clipped, preventing him from flying, he still would have the burning desire to mount up on wings and ascend into the sky. His ability, however, would be so impaired that he could never lift off the ground. He could not be true to his nature.

Such is the plight of humanity. We are born to ascend into the very environment of God's presence where we belong; but something has clipped our wings, disabling us from responding to the cry from within. "Deep calleth unto deep at the noise of thy waterspouts: all thy waves and thy billows are gone over me" (Ps. 42:7). Because man is shut out of the presence of God, he suffers many maladies.

## Hindrances to God's Presence

The greatest hindrance, of course, is the fact that God is unapproachable. Sin has created an unmanageable debt for all humanity. The good news, however, is that Christ has paid the debt and bridged that gap to God for all. But there are still at least three challenges that stand in man's way as he strives after God's presence.

### The Moral Bankruptcy of the Human Soul

The first obstruction is the moral bankruptcy of the human soul. Man's inevitable striking against the kingdom of God and the moral order of the universe puts him in debt to that moral order and becomes a debt to the great God who created the heavens and earth. This debt must be paid. What the moral conscience of all men requires and cries out for is a fund of merit sufficient to pay that debt. That's why every religion tries to establish this fund of merit but without success.

Religion does it through what is referred to as "good works," resulting in emptiness and a deep-seated sense of guilt that nothing can wash away. But even if such a fund of merit could be achieved, it would not be enough. Pardon must be secured.

What if some lowlife criminal desired to have an audience with the queen of England? Someone with a long-time record of criminal activity desired to stand before the gracious queen and be admitted into her presence.

Such a matter could be arranged, because many have so desired and been welcomed there. But something would have to be done before that criminal could be admitted into the presence of the queen. Nobody could arbitrarily admit a criminal into the queen's presence—could admit someone who by his previous acts jeopardizes the safety of her gracious majesty and all that she symbolizes.

Through the years, many have gone through the legal protocol to prepare them for an audience with the queen. The primary ingredient for entering the queen's presence would rest on a legal pardon. Somebody would have to straighten out all the legal issues necessary to grant a full pardon. The debt would have to be paid. Pardon is a legal act beyond the capabilities of the person being pardoned; it is an outside force putting to rest the criminal's past. That would be the first step.

No criminal could capriciously come into the presence of the queen simply because he desired to do so. It would have to be someone who was yielding allegiance; but that would not be enough either. Even though the government could pardon this man—could strike from the record all criminal counts against him so that there was nothing on the books—and restore his citizenship as though he were a freeborn citizen once more, even that would not go far enough.

Now take this example of a criminal standing in the presence of the queen of England and think about our desire to enter the presence of holy God. The human heart knows that it cannot enter into the presence of God, because it has rebelled against God. There must be something done to make it possible for that rebellion to end and be forgiven. The act of rebellion must be pardoned completely, and the rebel restored to full citizenship in the kingdom of God, to be made a child of the Father.

All of that was done in Christ. But that is still not enough. There is another hindrance.

## The Foul Scent of Sin Upon Us

Let's return to the example of a criminal wanting an audience with the queen. Although the man has been fully pardoned of his crimes, and his past has been expunged, that is not enough. Not only must the past be dealt with, but also the present must be attended to. He could not just walk off Skid Row, unshaven and dirty, into the presence of the queen. He would also have to be washed and made fit to stand in the queen's presence. This pardoned man is dirty, smelly and unshaven. Before going into the presence of the queen, he would have to be groomed and cleansed and properly dressed.

If he is to stand in the queen's presence, his present condition and attire must be in complete conformity to her wishes and demands. She sets the standard, and all who come into her presence must conform to it. She never conforms to their standard.

In like fashion, man cannot enter the presence of God with the foul scent of sin upon him. Although the past has been dealt with, the present condition also must be addressed. The very presence of sinful thoughts, for example, inhibits our approach into the presence of God. The filth clinging to our robe of self-righteousness repulses the pure, undefiled presence of God. Not only do we need a change of heart, but we also need a change of garment. Therefore, we must exchange our filthy garment for the pure robe of righteousness. To come into the presence of God, we must conform in every way to His standard.

In light of this standard, some provision must be made available. Some fountain must be opened in the House of David for sin and uncleanness so that we may not only be forgiven but also cleansed. The blood of Jesus Christ accomplished this stupendous act! This is what Christianity teaches. This is the witness the Church gives to the world. Man's moral conscience, crying for pardon and cleansing before the presence of the great God, has now found it by an event, an act of the eternal Son, who is the image of the invisible God and the firstborn of every creature, upholding all things by the Word of His power (see Col. 1:15-17). He turned aside to do this awful act—this awesome, amazing, stupendous act—by Himself. He single-handedly purged our sins. He alone could do it, so He did it alone.

In other things, Jesus Christ willingly accepted help. When He was to be born into the world, He accepted the help of the Virgin Mary, who gave her pure body to God and brought Him into the world—a man born a babe in Bethlehem's manger. He wept in her arms, nursed at her breast, was taken care of and fed and loved. He accepted the help of His mother. He willingly accepted help from Joseph, His supposed father, a simple carpenter who worked from sunup to sundown to provide clothing and shelter for his wife and the boy, Jesus.

But in this one area—the purging of man's sin—the Son operated alone and single-handedly fulfilled all the requirements for man's redemption. Therefore, the foul scent of sin upon man can be washed and cleansed by the blood Jesus Christ shed on the cross. This standard allows us to come boldly into the presence of God.

## The Lost Concept of Majesty

Even those in Christendom have been challenged in their striving after God. Not only our garments, but also our attitudes and intentions need divine purification. We must come into His presence in a way that is worthy of Him.

The present generation of Christians has suffered what I call the lost concept of majesty. This has come about by a slow decline, manifesting itself in our depreciation of ourselves. Those who hold a low value of man have a corresponding low value of God. After all, God created man in His own image. When we cease to understand the majestic nature of man, we cease to appreciate the majesty of God. How did we get to this place?

At one time, many believed the earth was the center of the universe and all the heavenly bodies revolved around it. It was a simple earth and easy to explain, because we go by our sight, and by our sight the earth is still, and everything is traveling around it. Most people believed this until the time of Copernicus and Galileo, who came along in the sixteenth century and taught that the earth is not fixed at all, but in motion around an orbit.

For the most part, people complied with those findings and said, "Then, we're all wrong about anything being fixed. We don't believe in it anymore." So they stopped believing there was anything fixed in the heavens, or at least that the earth was fixed.

The common thought at the time was, "We're riding around on earth's diurnal course. If the earth is not the center of the world, man is the center of God's creation. Surely not only the center, but the top of God's creation." The accepted belief at the time was that man is the top of the world; God made him, and made him in His image.

In time, Charles Darwin came along and taught that man is not the center, the head, the top and the final, finished product of the creation. Furthermore, the earth and all that is in it and on it is not a creation at all; it just happens to be here. It is simply a moving purpose. Man is simply partway up from where he used to be and where he is going to be. Man once moved about in colloidal ooze and crept and sloshed about in the depths of the sea. Then the sun struck him and he took on an eye and became a mudpuppy. He moved some more, and after the passing of a few more million years, he became a bird. Then after that, he became a monkey, and we are on our way, and here we are now. However, we are not where we are going and we are not where we have been. We are not the center of anything. We are simply taking off. We are in motion.

About the turn of the twentieth century, or a little before, the world suddenly drew a deep breath and said, "Can it possibly be that we are struggling upward and what used to be called sin is not sin at all? It is something else. It is simply the residual twitching of the old mudpuppy. The lingering remnants of that which used to be in the man, and little by little, we are purging him out. Look at that baboon, and look at that college professor. What an amazing difference! Look at him sit there with a dreamy look on his face while he listens to a Beethoven symphony. See how far he's come?"

Yes, he certainly has come a long way. See him two nights later when his wife bawls him out and he turns on her, shoots her, stabs her or walks out on her. He is a human being, too, and not all of his degrees have changed him on any level.

In spite of all this, there were people saying, "Somewhere there's something fixed. If it is not the earth, it is the sun." About this time, Albert Einstein came along and said, "That is not the way it is at all. Nothing is fixed anywhere, not even the sun. The sun is simply another star, and around it has gathered the solar system, but that is not fixed either. It is moving around another star farther out, and then that whole thing is moving around another big one still farther out."

By this time, your head begins to ache, and you say, "Please, leave me alone. I can't take this." All of these postulations have served to take away every idea concerning the majesty of man. You cannot believe any of these things and then look at a man with any respect.

Look at the pictures of our founders and forbears—very dignified old gentlemen they are, but you cannot look on them with respect if you've lost the sense of the majesty of man because God created him. You would see under their sideburns the marks of the mudpuppy gills. And you would realize they are not dignified men made in the image of God at all but had crept up that far, out of the gutter.

This is what this world system wants us to believe, taking away all sense of majesty. You could not possibly respect that which crawled up from below.

A sense of majesty has been lost, and along with this a sense of dignity has disappeared among mankind. This has so permeated our society that it is perhaps beyond reclaiming.

Even Christians suffer with a demoralized sense of majesty. It does not matter whether it is true or not as long as it is funny. We do not care whether it is truth or not if it is said in a cute way that entertains us.

But I believe the Majesty is still in the heavens. This Majesty still sits on His throne before which angels, archangels, seraphim and cherubim continue to cry, "Holy, holy, holy, Lord God of Sabbaoth." When Jesus, who was God by Himself, alone purged our sins, He went back and sat down where He had been through the long, long ages—at the right hand of the Majesty in the heavens. After He sat down on that right hand, the eternal Son turned to man.

## Reclaiming Our Sense of the Majesty on High

Christian leadership today has done so much to hinder the majestic elements of Christianity. Everything must have some kind of a logical, rational explanation. I readily admit that it verges on the impossible to describe in any degree of adequacy the conscious, manifest presence of God. Any lame attempt on my part will crumble in frustrated disappointment. The best I possibly can hope is to put forth my personal experience backed up by scriptural exhortation. My part is only to whet the appetite and then trust the Holy Spirit to take it from there.

Many people like their religion in a nice neat formula— something they can do without much effort or thought. These days everybody has some shortcut into the blessings of God's presence: "Five easy steps to happiness" or "Ten easy steps to get everything you want from God." However, there is no nice neat formula for this. Rather, we need to whet the spiritual appetite for that which it truly craves: the presence of God. I know well that if you can explain it, it certainly is not the majestic presence of God.

Most people, unfortunately, would pursue these pages with a sense of curiosity and soon grow bored and turn aside for the titillation of some new thing. Becoming fascinated with some exterior trinket, they soon lose interest in pursuing the presence of God. For those, someone always comes along boasting of some new religious gadget to play with. The poor, undernourished, immature Christian goes from one religious gadget to another, ending up with an emptiness inside that they cannot comprehend.

This book is a small attempt to fan the flame of holy desire toward God. I hope you will catch the passion and press forward to delight in the conscious, manifest presence of God. Thomas à Kempis understood this and wrote, "If you are to live an interior life you must learn to enjoy His intimacy, unhampered by any interruption from the world outside." He expands this thought in his book *The Imitation of Christ:* "For a man to make real spiritual progress, he must deny himself; a man who has made this renunciation enjoys great freedom and security."[1]

Unfortunately, the world is too much with us, and it has successfully become entrenched upon our inner soul, making it unable to court His presence. The good news is that the heart of man truly hungers for God's presence and that all of the great barriers prohibiting that striving after God have been overcome in Jesus Christ.

# God Is Present Everywhere
### by Oliver Holden (1765–1844)

They who seek the throne of grace
Find that throne in every place;
If we live a life of prayer,
God is present everywhere.

In our sickness and our health,
In our want, or in our wealth,
If we look to God in prayer,
God is present everywhere.

When our earthly comforts fail,
When the woes of life prevail,
'Tis the time for earnest prayer;
God is present everywhere.

Then, my soul, in every strait,
To thy Father come, and wait;
He will answer every prayer:
God is present everywhere.

**Note**

1. Thomas à Kempis, *The Imitation of Christ*, translated by Ronald Knox and Michael Oakley (New York: Sheed & Ward, Inc., 1959).

# 2

# HINDRANCES ON THE PATHWAY TO GOD'S PRESENCE

*Therefore we ought to give the more earnest heed to the things which we have heard, lest at any time we should let them slip. For if the word spoken by angels was stedfast, and every transgression and disobedience received a just recompence of reward; how shall we escape, if we neglect so great salvation; which at the first began to be spoken by the Lord, and was confirmed unto us by them that heard him; God also bearing them witness, both with signs and wonders, and with divers miracles, and gifts of the Holy Ghost, according to his own will?*

HEBREWS 2:1-4

We have already established that deep within the soul of humanity is a latent desire to come into God's presence. But that desire, put there by God, is not enough to overcome the hindrances that block the pathway. Although the hindrances are many, the main obstruction into God's presence is the unredeemed nature of man.

To worship God from the depths of the human soul is to discover worship in its purest form, unaffected by the world around; and it is deeper than any mere human emotion. For the unbeliever, worshiping God is impossible. The sin nature is repelled by the purity of God's nature, and seeks other consolations. These two natures are incompatible, which is the practical outcome of alienation from God.

Even the believer experiences obstacles that challenge his pursuit of God. The greatest challenge facing every Christian is to overcome these hindrances on the path to God's presence. The enemy of man's soul, however, is determined to make the pathway as virtually impossible to travel as he can. For the most part, he has done a great job of discouraging pilgrims in their quest for God's presence.

John, the Beloved, understood this and encourages us with these words: "Ye are of God, little children, and have overcome them: because greater is he that is in you, than he that is in the world" (1 John 4:4). Certainly, the opposition is there and it is real, but it is not of such a nature as to keep us from God's presence. We can overcome all the wiles of the enemy and anything he puts in our way.

The most important thing we can devote ourselves to is giving attention to the things of God to save our soul. This must be an active, persistent and deliberate intent on our part, regardless of the difficulties that lie in our path.

Too many people have made coming into God's presence not only complicated but also all but unattainable, discouraging many from trying. It is not a journey for the indolent or for those addicted to entertainment and the coarse pleasures of the flesh.

The fact that there are hindrances only emphasizes the value of coming into God's presence. If experiencing His presence were without obstruction, it would be without enticement as well. Someone has well said that whatever is without cost does not have value. When we think of coming into the presence of God, what could be more valuable than that? Certainly, the importance of coming into God's presence is worth overcoming every obstacle along the way.

Wouldn't you think that something so attractive would be at the forefront of every inquiring human being's desire? There are stumbling blocks along the way, however, that are of such a nature as to keep out all but those who have an impassioned desire for the presence of God—a desire stronger than the draw of anything else in life.

Penetrating the holy presence of God is the reward of fighting the good fight and overcoming all obstructions in the way. This all-consuming desire for God's presence goes a long way in tackling the major hindrances a seeker might find. When the goal is in clear view, the obstacles become trivial. Let's take a look at the main obstacles that can keep us from pursuing God and see how we can move around them.

## Manmade Errors

Perhaps the greatest obstacle preventing us from coming into God's presence would be the errors propagated down the years. People have not come right out and said them in so many words, but they think them. And what we think, so are we.

### Error: All Religions Lead to God

One manmade error is thinking that there are any number of religions that are good in varying degrees. Therefore, why should we give the more earnest heed to the message of Christianity? Well, God has spoken through His Son and said, "Hear ye Him." And Moses said, "This is that Moses, which said unto the children of Israel, A prophet shall the Lord your God raise up unto you of your brethren, like unto me; him shall ye hear" (Acts 7:37). Jesus Christ is not another teacher; He is the final teacher and the last Word of God to men. What He has said closes all other arguments.

## Error: Man Has No Spiritual Responsibility

Another manmade error is the belief that there is nothing to be disturbed about because Christ carries the supreme authority of God. Therefore, everything is taken care of and we don't need to be bothered.

Christ does carry the supreme authority of God; but to ignore that authority is a grave offense. Some will say, "God will take the initiative; I do not need to do anything. I believe that God will always be the aggressor." By the way, I believe that, too; but remember, God has already taken the initiative when He sent His holy Son, Jesus Christ, into the world, and when He sent the Holy Spirit down to take the things of Christ and show them unto us. So God has already taken the initiative. If God cannot disturb us, He cannot move us. If He cannot move us, He cannot save us. If He cannot get us concerned about the things of God, He cannot do anything at all for us.

## Error: The Message Needs to Be Palatable

John and Charles Wesley were men with a deep concern for the seriousness of spiritual matters. We sing the Wesley hymns about being concerned and moved, but we do not half mean them. We ought to mean them, because we ought to give them the more earnest heed, which means careful attention. We ought to read. We ought to listen. We ought to search. We ought to examine and reexamine. And it ought to be done in earnest. We ought to put away levity, flippancy and fun.

The curse of everything today is that it has to be funny. If it is not funny, it is not popular. But there is nothing funny in God seeing His race wander away in the night. There was nothing funny about His sending His holy Son to be born of the virgin. There was nothing funny about His persecution and crucifixion. There was nothing funny about the coming of the Holy Ghost; nothing funny about the judgment and the resurrection of the wicked dead. Levity, flippancy or fun has no place when we consider the things of God. We ought to give the more earnest heed to the things that we have heard.

The great labor of the Church has always been to get people to give serious attention to spiritual matters. A great many pastors and preachers do not worry about this at all, because they do not expect anything and, therefore, they do not get it. But a man of God, with the burden of the Holy Spirit on him, will want to stir the people to serious attention. Until serious attention has been given to the claims of Christ, it is for us as if the Bible had never been written.

Medicine sitting on the shelf and never taken has never cured anybody. Food left in the refrigerator and never eaten has never nourished anybody. Heat not turned on has never warmed anybody. And the Bible itself, though it is nourishment, though it is light, though it is warmth, though it is medicine to the soul, yet it never helps anybody where there is not serious attention given to it. And when we do not give serious attention, it is as if Christ had not come into the world and died for mankind. He might as well have not come and died as for us to neglect all that is meant by His coming and dying.

## The Curse of Our Contemporary Culture

Every Christian faces some hindrance in seeking the presence of God. Contemporary Christianity is so taken up by the world that pressing on to the deep things of God becomes rather difficult. Our contemporary times stand in the way of anybody taking his or her spiritual life seriously. So many things are thrown at us; it takes a very resilient soul to resist the onslaught.

Perhaps the most dangerous situation confronting Christians today is what I call *cauterizing the conscience*. That is, making a person insensitive or callous to the world around him. In practical terms, he experiences a deadening of feelings toward morals. Quite simply, this *moral insensibility* is a lack of feeling. You cannot feel the whole moral question. The strange paradox is that a person may be troubled by his inability to feel, yet he cannot feel. Even among those who consider themselves Christians, there is very little outrage at the immorality of our times.

The source of this dangerous condition is the semi-anesthetization caused by the act of sinning. When a person sins, he anesthetizes his conscience, to a certain extent. I call this the *cauterizing of the conscience*. If you cauterize a thing, it will hurt at first, but after it heals over, you have no feeling there. Where the cauterization took place, there will develop a hard shell, a thick skin. Sin does that. It cauterizes the conscience, and soon it does not bother us that we are sinning. This is the work of the blinding agent of the unholy one we call the devil. I do believe in the devil and that he blinds the minds of those who believe not, lest the light of the glorious gospel of Christ might shine onto them (see 2 Cor. 4:4).

Then there is *spiritual lethargy*, an unnatural inward drowsiness when faced with the claims of God. Yet, we hear a speech on the dangers of our times and we immediately want to know how we can get to a fallout shelter. We hear a program on cancer, and we examine ourselves and wonder if that last pain was a cancer. We are always concerned about superficial things but rarely concerned about spiritual things.

Thomas à Kempis wisely observed, "We give all our attention to things that do us little good, or none at all; things that are vitally necessary we don't bother about them, just give them the go-by. Yes, all that goes to make man drives him to meddle with outward things, and if he doesn't soon recover his senses, is only too glad to wallow in material interests and pleasures."[1]

*Moral insensitivity* and *spiritual lethargy* are two great curses because they keep us from taking earnest heed to our spiritual health. Unless we are serious about our approach to God, we will be hindered every step of the way. These two things can only be corrected by a sound conversion to Jesus Christ.

## Giving God Leftovers

Then there is the preoccupation with making a living. Jesus called it the "cares of this life" (see Matt. 13:22). If everyone would put as much earnest time and give as much serious attention to seeking God as they put into making a living, they would become a much finer Christian, and soon people would wonder what happened. If women would give as much earnest heed to the claims of Christ and to the needs of their own soul as they give to their house, their cooking and their family, at the end of the week they would have made such spiritual advances that they would be ashamed of the way they had been living before.

The simple fact is that God gets the leftovers, never the main meal. God never gets anything new. He gets the hand-me-downs. We give to God that which we do not need instead of giving to Him that which we need, and thus earning a crown for ourselves. If we were as concerned with our spiritual condition as we are with our homes and our businesses and our income, we would go forward spiritually at a great rate. The beautiful thing about it is that we would not neglect our homes to do it, and we would not neglect our businesses to do it. You do not have to choose between making a living and going forward with God. You can do both. There is time to do both. You do not have to choose between keeping your house decent and cooking your meals for your husband, and going on with God. You can do both.

An excellent example was a woman by the name of Susannah Wesley, who had 19 children. John Wesley was the eighteenth child. She kept that house spic and span and was known as one of the greatest women of faith of her time. She decided she could look after her family and still make spiritual progress. Her domestic duties did not distract her in the least from her spiritual pursuits.

The same goes for students. If they would seek the face of God as earnestly as they seek books, they would find themselves growing in grace like grass by the watercourses.

## Constantly Seeking After Pleasure

Another hindrance is the constant seeking after pleasure. There are the physical pleasures: comforts, various vices, food and the rest. And there are mental pleasures, such as social pleasures, gambling and amusements and the reading of fiction. There are aesthetic pleasures: art, music, higher learning and sophisticated culture. All these put together simply give pleasant sensations, the same sensation a baby gets by sucking his thumb. The whole human race has simply grown up seeking pleasure so that we are a race of grownup thumb-suckers. We give over our time to acquiring a pleasant sensation when we ought to give over our time to the advancing of our souls.

Peter says, "Save yourselves from this untoward generation" (Acts 2:40). We may not be in earnest, but God is in dead earnest. God, the Father, was in earnest when He planned and finally accomplished the work of redemption. God, the Son, was in earnest when He sweat great drops of blood in the garden of Gethsemane. And God, the Holy Ghost, is always in earnest when He comes to dwell in the nature of men. We ought to give the more earnest heed lest we drift away from it; lest we should let it slip. If you will notice in the margin of some Bibles, it says, "Lest that anytime we should let them slip" and "run out as a leaking vessel." Other versions have "we should drift away from it." A great many people have leaking hearts and spirits.

## Letting Truth Leak from Our Heart

We neglect "so great salvation" by drifting from it. And how do we neglect it? We get the truth in our heart, but we let it leak away. It is a heartbreaking truth that some hearts are leaky, and their good resolutions all trickle away.

People remain sober until New Year's and then on New Year's Eve, they lose their sobriety and start making resolutions. "I resolve that I will be kinder to my wife this year." "I resolve that I will give regularly to the church." "I resolve that I will pray regularly every day." "I resolve that I will not let a day go by that I do not read the Holy Scriptures." "I resolve that I will seek to know God better." "I resolve . . ."

But the heart is a leaky thing, and before the first of February, the average person's resolutions have all evaporated. The good intentions, the strong wine of spiritual desire when you heard a man preach whose words touched you particularly; suddenly you can see the strong desire for God. And you long after the strong wine of spiritual desire, but your heart is like a sieve, and pretty soon it all leaks away. Soon there is no desire left at all.

The difference between spiritual things and earthly things is that the things of the spirit are so modest; the things of the spirit are not pushing in on you; they are not singing commercials to you; they are not knocking on your door and urging you to buy; they are simply waiting for you to notice.

Jesus did not lift up His voice nor make Himself heard in the street. He did not cry aloud, but was calm and quiet. People came to Him for the truth. But the things of the flesh are so insistent, so clamorous. Before you are up in the morning, they are clamoring at you, trying to get you interested in buying what they are selling or doing what they have decided you should do. Everybody is singing to you, urging you, pushing you—by example, by precept, by instruction, by advertising and urging—trying to get you to go certain ways and do certain things.

Our Lord is never intrusive; but the things of the world are intrusive. Here is the point I am trying to make: If you are going to give attention to the things of God and save your own soul, you are going to have to have a good intention, a good resolution and then see to it that you do it. Do not let the devil prevent you. You are going to have to take yourself by the scruff of the neck, shake yourself and say, "Now, I don't know what others are going to do, but as for me, I'm going to seek the face of God. I'm going to see if I can be a better man next week than I was last week, and a better man next month than I was last month."

God meant it when He gave us the Law. Christ meant it when He died and rose on the third day. The Holy Ghost means it when He quietly speaks to your heart. How much more will we be judged if we heed not the truth that they were judged that heeded not the Law? "For if the word spoken by angels was stedfast, and every transgression and disobedience received a just recompense of reward; how shall we escape, if we neglect so great salvation; which at the first began to be spoken by the Lord, and was confirmed unto us by them that heard him; God also bearing them witness, both with signs and wonders, and with divers miracles, and gifts of the Holy Ghost, according to his own will?" (Heb. 2:2-4).

Some confess, "I intended to . . . later." However, there was no later time.

"I didn't understand," they say. But they understood enough at the time.

"I was too busy." But at last they found time to die.

Somebody else says, "Nobody in my crowd paid any attention to these things," but it is always so. The saving voice of God speaks to a crowd of men, but only one here and there hears it. When the voice of God spoke to the antediluvian world, only Noah and his family heard it. The rest of them perished in the flood.

Somebody else says, "If I pay attention to this, I'll lose my job." Chances are, you will not, but if you do, any job you lose saving your soul certainly will be a wonderful bargain. Somebody else says, "I want to have some fun yet. And then I'll become a Christian." I will not answer that. It is too meaningless, too lacking in significance to warrant any serious answer. Another says, "I was afraid of what people would say." Afraid of what *people* would say? What about what God says?

Society is in an elaborate conspiracy to make us alike. Society is in a conspiracy to make us all bad; not too bad, because if we get too bad, we become a problem to the police. But not too good, for if we get too good, we are fanatical, so they say. So society wants to keep us nice, trimmed down, going to church, supporting boys' clubs and girls' clubs and hospitals. Certainly those things are all right. The general society wants to keep us just good enough not to be a problem to the police but bad enough not to bother their conscience.

I hear the voice of God calling us to a higher kind of life. The book of Hebrews is an urgent, vibrant, living book that speaks to those that are on the border and says, "Go on over. You can dare to do it. Go on over." And it speaks to those who could not quite make up their minds whether they wanted to obey and believe God, and says, "You dare obey. You dare believe."

Whatever causes us to overcome all hindrances is handsomely rewarded when we break through to the glorious sunshine of His blessed presence.

## Love Divine, All Love Excelling
### by Charles Wesley (1707–1788)

Love divine, all love excelling,
Joy of heaven, to earth come down;
Fix in us thy humble dwelling;
All thy faithful mercies crown.
Jesus, thou art all compassion,
Pure, unbounded love thou art;
Visit us with thy salvation,
Enter every trembling heart.

Breathe, oh, breathe thy Holy Spirit
Into every troubled breast;
Let us all thy grace inherit;
Let us find thy promised rest;
Take away the love of sinning;
Take our load of guilt away;
End the work of thy beginning;
Bring us to eternal day.

Carry on thy new creation;
Pure and holy may we be;
Let us see our whole salvation

Perfectly secured by thee;
Change from glory into glory,
Till in heaven we take our place,
Till we cast our crowns before thee,
Lost in wonder, love, and praise.

**Note**

1. Thomas à Kempis, *The Imitation of Christ*, translated by Ronald Knox and Michael Oakley (New York: Sheed & Ward, Inc., 1959).

# 3

# MAN IS NATURALLY DRAWN TOWARD GOD'S PRESENCE

*But we see Jesus, who was made a little lower than the angels
for the suffering of death, crowned with glory and honour; that he by
the grace of God should taste death for every man. For it became him,
for whom are all things, and by whom are all things, in bringing
many sons unto glory, to make the captain of their salvation
perfect through sufferings.*

HEBREWS 2:9-10

Of all God's creation, man is the only creature implanted with spiritual aspirations, leading him to prayer and worship. Wherever you find man, you will find him engaged in some sort of worship. No mistake about it, something within the creature lifts itself up in response to something within the Creator. That "something" is the great mystery of the human heart created in the image of God.

If a culture does not know the true Jesus Christ, it will invent its own God and worship that. The history of the world is filled with religions conquering countries. It would be impossible to find any culture in any generation in any part of the world that does not have some kind of religious tendencies and rituals. Where did that come from? Why is it that man is always looking upwards or at least outward from himself to something greater and more magnificent than himself?

These spiritual stirrings within the natural heart fall on deaf ears and go unanswered for one simple reason. From a mere intellectual and rational viewpoint, they are incomprehensible. Man feels drawn toward something but does not know what it is or how to define it. It is something above and beyond human rationalizing.

Down through history man has taken many paths in his quest for God's presence, all to no avail. Only one path is correct, and that path is revealed in the Word of God. Only in the Bible do we begin to understand what these inward stirrings are and how to find entrance into the presence of God.

A right understanding of the Bible opens to us the only path into the presence of God.

## The Bible Way into God's Presence

Two aspects of the Bible that are critical to coming into God's presence are *revelation* and *inspiration*.

In the volumes of Christian testimony that have come down through the centuries, there are two words that occur frequently: one is "inspiration," and the other is "revelation." When we say "inspiration," meaning that the Scripture is inspired or given by inspiration, we mean that in its original signature, that is, as originally given, the Holy Spirit inspired the Bible to be written. What we have was put down at the order of the Holy Spirit. That is what we mean by inspiration.

God wrote the Bible as originally given, and it is a trustworthy sourcebook of authentic truth. What we have in the Bible is true, but not everything that is true is in the Bible. You can learn everything from the Bible that the Bible teaches, but you cannot learn everything from the Bible, for the reason that the Bible does not teach everything. It does not pretend to. We must distinguish between *revealed truth* and *truth*.

## Revealed Truth

The Bible has to do with that which deals with redemption. It is a book interested in our rescue from sin, our moral rehabilitation and our spiritual regeneration. It is interested in keeping us right and making us useful and causing us to grow up into the maturity of a Christian. Then, at last, it is interested in preparing us for the journey across from this temporal life to eternity. It is interested in all that, but it is not interested in geometry. You cannot go to the Bible and learn geometry, but you can go to the Bible and learn that "God so loved the world, that he gave his only begotten Son" (John 3:16). You cannot learn from the Bible how to bake a pie or send up a rocket. But you can learn from the Bible that "except a man be born again, he cannot see the kingdom of God" (John 3:3).

The Bible reveals the truth we need to know to save us from sin, to regenerate us, to rehabilitate us morally and spiritually, and to prepare us for the day of the Lord. It is all in the Word, and that is what we mean when we say the Bible is the only sourcebook for our rule and practice. The Bible is the only final, authentic sourcebook of information concerning those things that have to do with our salvation.

The Scriptures tell us that God created the heavens and the earth. In addition, we are told many other things that do not seem to bear directly upon our salvation, but that do, nevertheless, bear upon it. Revelation is the uncovering of truths that had not been known before and are undiscoverable.

## Discoverable Truth

Some things you can discover on your own. For example, someone discovered the atom. Roman philosopher Titus Lucretius Carus (ca. 99 BC–ca. 55 BC) wrote a book before Christ's time, *On the Nature of Things*, and in it, he explained about atoms. He thought atoms were tiny, hard bits of matter out of which everything was made, just as a concrete building is made out of tiny bits of matter: sand and concrete. You can break it down and find its tiny particles. He came wonderfully close to it, even though he did not have the benefit of modern scientific techniques and information.

Those things are discoverable. You can discover them. This is a distinction between "revealed truth" and "truth." There are truths that can never be discovered on their own or by man's initiative. God inspired the Bible to be written, and inspires man to say things; often those things could be discovered. For example, look at Psalm 8:3-8:

> When I consider thy heavens, the work of thy fingers, the moon and the stars, which thou hast ordained; what is man, that thou art mindful of him? and the son of man, that thou visitest him? For thou hast made him a little lower than the angels, and hast crowned

him with glory and honour. Thou madest him to have dominion over the works of thy hands; thou hast put all things under his feet: All sheep and oxen, yea, and the beasts of the field; the fowl of the air, and the fish of the sea.

Those words were an inspired utterance. The Spirit of God moved David to write this psalm, and it has a spiritual benefit for us. But this is not revelation, because it is a reaction anybody could have, even if he were an atheist. He could still look up into the heavens and say, "When I look at all of that space, what is man?"

Notice that Psalm 8 is a night scene, while Psalm 19 is a day scene:

The heavens declare the glory of God; and the firmament sheweth his handywork. Day unto day uttereth speech, and night unto night sheweth knowledge (Ps. 19:1-2).

And then in verse 5, the psalmist talks about the sun and says, "Which is as a bridegroom coming out of his chamber, and rejoiceth as a strong man to run a race" (Ps. 19:5). Seen from the earth up, that is exactly what the sun looks like—a great, shining bridegroom of the world, shining in his splendor. Both psalms are inspired, but there is no particular revelation, because anybody could say the same thing. Anybody could say that the "heavens declared God's glory and the firmament showed His handiwork." That is a discoverable truth.

## The Main Difference Between Man and Every Other Creature

Everything in the natural world falls short of man's supreme aspiration for God and His presence. You do not have to like it, but we might as well face up to it: We are the glory and the rubbish of the universe; but we never would have been the rubbish of the universe if we had not chosen the gutter. If sin had not entered the world, and we had not fallen, we would never have been the rubbish of the universe. We would have been the glory of the universe. When our Lord is finished with His redemptive work, He will have made His people, once again, the glory of the universe when He comes to be admired in His saints and glorified in all them that see Him.

Man is the weakest creature there is, but he is the only creature that knows how weak he is. That is where his glory lies: in his weakness. He is able to know how weak he is, and no other creature knows this.

I do not suppose that if you were to ask a mosquito, "Are you weak?" he would say yes. He does not know he is weak. He could not answer you. He would not know what you said. If mosquitoes could talk, they would call us the animal that swats, because that is the only thing they know about us.

Man is the unknown—pitiful, wonderful, weak, mysterious—and yet he is the only creature that knows he is this. Man is the only creature that sins, and yet he is the only creature that could know that he sins. And man is the only creature that knows how foolish and inconsistent he is, and he laughs at himself. He is the only creature that aspires, because there is no other creature dissatisfied with himself. Man alone is dissatisfied with himself.

In John Keats's poem "Ode to a Nightingale," he made this point, among other very wonderful things: You were here. You were here way back long ago when the Grecians heard thee sing among the isles of Greece. Yes, the nightingale was there then, but the nightingale was there before there was any Greece, and before there was any Egypt. Why has the nightingale remained the nightingale from the time God created her and said, "Let the birds inhabit the air"? Because the nightingale, although she is a beautiful singer, does not aspire. But the man who used to come out of his cave and listen to a nightingale is now dressed in a Hart, Schaffner & Marx suit and watches television. Why? He has aspired, you see. He has come up. Only man aspires. All other creatures are exactly what they were; the only creature that ever improves is the one that man gets hold of and crossbreeds.

Those Guernsey, Jersey, Holstein and Hereford cattle you see standing around in little clusters under the trees on hot days are crossbreeds. They have been bred up to that. Someone got a hold of a poor swayback heifer and bred her to something better. Then he bred that to something better, and on until he has these fine cattle. If man can get hold of a thing, he will breed it up, because man alone aspires. Nothing else aspires. The lowly cow does not aspire to be anything more or else than she is.

What does this indicate? It indicates that God made man in His own image, and in the image and likeness of God made He him, and of nothing else can this be said.

Therefore, man aspires and is the only creature that prays and worships. God made man to worship, and he is the only creature that God made to worship, at least the only creature down here. The lion roars for his prey and the bird builds its nest in the thickets. The stormy wind fulfills God's will, and He gives hail and snow like wool. Snow does not pray, and neither does the bird pray; neither does the lion pray, and neither does the stormy wind pray. We can read prayer into it, but it is not there until we read it in. We, who can pray, read into nature prayers, and we say the wind is moaning her prayers to heaven, but she is only moaning in our imagination. The wind is just blowing. You and I are doing the moaning. So we read those thoughts into nature.

We say the little bird dips his bill in the water, then looks up and thanks God for it, but the bird is merely putting his chin up so the water will run down. That is all, purely a mechanical thing. No bird prays. I think it is perfectly terrible to get a dog down beside the bed and have him pray, as some people do. If God made a dog to pray, he would be praying without your getting him down alongside your bed, so stop it if you have been doing it. No dog ever prayed. No bird ever prayed. It is man alone that prays.

## "What Is Man That Thou Art Mindful of Him?"

In the vastness of the universe, man is very small indeed. But seen as a spiritual creature in the bosom of God, he is greater than all the winds that blow and all the mountains that rise and all the seas that flow and all the rivers that run down to the sea. He is greater, because God made him in His own image. That is why the Son came.

Why did the eternal Son become the Son of Man? He was the Son of God. So why did He become the Son of Man? He came for the singular reason that man had sinned and had become the glory and the rubbish of the universe. He came down in human flesh to get down as far as we were. If He had come into the world as a child of 10, there would have been 10 years unaccounted. If He had come as a child of five, there would have been five years unaccounted. If He had started at a year old, there would have been a year unaccounted. If He had been born by some miracle apart from childbirth, there would have been nine months unaccounted. Scripture says, "Therefore also that holy thing which shall be born of thee shall be called the Son of God" (Luke 1:35). Jesus went back not only to the original embryo, but all the way back to the original germ, that He might know everything that man knows and develop the way of man's development right up to full, blooming manhood.

Jesus came down to where we are. If He had been born in a palace, there might have been those who were born in huts and grass cottages that He would not have understood; but He was born in a stable that He might know the poorest there are.

## Revealed Truth Allows Us to Live by Faith

Revealed truth leads to a restoration of God's sovereignty in the redeemed. Christ is now the corporeal head of the human race, and under Him, the human race is going to regain sovereignty. Christ came down in order that He might taste death for every man. That word "taste" does not mean taste as a child might taste food and then reject it. It means "experience." He experienced death for every man. "Now we see not yet all things put under him" (Heb. 2:8), but we see only that which has been done. We see that He was born. We see that He grew to manhood. We see that He died. We see that He rose again from the dead. We see that He is saving His Church and that there is a Church within the church; there are redeemed people, regenerated people, bloodwashed people, forgiven people—people who compose the true Church. That is the Church inside the false church—the Church that God acknowledges and approves within the vast Christendom, which God rejects.

We do not yet see all things put under His feet, but we do see what was done. By faith, we see all things put under Him. Faith is a kind of sight, because faith sees what has not yet happened. And if we have actual faith, we act as if we see what we believe. And if we claim we believe and do not have faith, we act as if we believe it but do not believe it at all. We say we believe in revelation. We believe in inspiration. We believe that man is made in the image of God. We believe that God was made in the image of man by the incarnation of the holy Son. We say we believe He tasted death for every man that we might cease to be the disgrace of the universe and become the glory of the universe again. And if we truly believe this, we begin to act as if we believe it, and it changes our inner perception.

Remember: You do not believe a thing rightly until you act in accordance with it. When you bring your life into line with your faith, you are a believer. But when your life is not in line with your faith, you are no true believer at all. We believe He tasted death for every man. We believe that He will soon triumph over all things, and God will put all things under His feet. I believe that, and I believe there will be a new heaven and a new earth, wherein dwells righteousness.

We see not all things under Him, but we see Jesus. God has put all things in subjection under His feet. For in that He put all in subjection under Him, He left nothing that is not put under Him. We do not see it all done yet, but we have faith, and we see Jesus, who for a little while was made lower than angels in order that He might suffer death. We see Him crowned with glory and honor at the right hand of God the Father Almighty. And when He comes back again, He will put all things under His feet.

For myself, with God's help, I want to live for that time. I want my money to live for that time. I want my talents, whatever they may be, to live for that time. I want my time to be given for that hour when He comes back again. I do not want to divide my life and live for the earth while this is approaching. I believe with all my heart that God has put all things under His feet, and one of these days, He is coming back to take His power and to reign. May God grant that you and I be ready.

Man's highest aspirations are fulfilled through the revealed truth of God's Word. This truth obeyed will prepare the heart to come into the presence of God in worship and fellowship.

## Come Hither, All Ye Weary Souls
### by Isaac Watts (1674-1748)

Come hither, all ye weary souls,
Ye heavy-laden sinners, come;
I'll give you rest from all your toils,
And raise you to my heavenly home.

They shall find rest who learn of me:
I'm of a meek and lowly mind;

But passion rages like the sea,
And pride is restless as the wind.

Blest is the man whose shoulders take
My yoke, and bear it with delight:
My yoke is easy to the neck;
My grace shall make the burden light.

Jesus, we come at thy command;
With faith and hope and humble zeal,
Resign our spirits to thy hand,
To mould and guide us at thy will.

# 4

# Our Personal Guide into God's Presence

*So also Christ glorified not himself to be made an high priest; but he that said unto him, Thou art my Son, to day have I begotten thee. As he saith also in another place, Thou art a priest for ever after the order of Melchisedec. Who in the days of his flesh, when he had offered up prayers and supplications with strong crying and tears unto him that was able to save him from death, and was heard in that he feared; though he were a Son, yet learned he obedience by the things which he suffered; and being made perfect, he became the author of eternal salvation unto all them that obey him; called of God an high priest after the order of Melchisedec.*

Hebrews 5:5-10

Delighting in God's presence is not a do-it-yourself project. The very delicate nature of it requires an experienced guide, someone who can maneuver us around obstacles and bring us into the sunlight of God's wonderful presence.

This brings us to the idea of the priesthood, which is ordained by God and fulfills an important spiritual function. The very nature of God's presence requires a skilled and qualified guide. That guide must be a qualified priest who can lead us boldly into the presence of God.

One of the major doctrines set forth in the book of Hebrews is the high priesthood of the eternal Son. Introduced in Hebrews 2:17, and in Hebrews 3:1, we are told to "consider the Apostle and High Priest of our profession." Again, it is mentioned in Hebrews 4:14 and in chapters 5, 6 and 7. The meaning is the high priesthood as God ordained it, and the fulfillment of that priesthood is by our Lord Jesus Christ.

## The Idea of Priesthood

Few things in religious circles are the source of more abuse than the priesthood. Every base, unworthy religion found throughout the world has the idea of a priesthood attached to it. The priestly rites throughout the various religions of the world have offended and shocked humanity, and the priests themselves have often been corrupt, cruel and hypocritical.

If you want to get the shock of your life, read the story of the religions of Mexico practiced by the Aztecs and the Toltecs. Twenty thousand human beings, for instance, were offered in sacrifice at the dedication of one temple. Twenty thousand human beings were stretched out on a slab alive and their hearts cut out with stone axes as sacrifices to the deaf and dumb god of the Toltecs and the Aztecs in the olden days in Mexico. The evil they did is unspeakable.

You do not have to go back far to find priests habitually lying around drunk. Numerous abuses have attached themselves to the idea of the priesthood. Some have been self-righteous and arrogant, and many intimidate and exploit their poor people. And yet the idea of a priesthood was not thought of first by man, but by God. It is dimly seen in the praying father who assumes responsibility for his family, who teaches them by example and precept, and who prays for them.

Job, in the Old Testament, was a good example of this. After his children had enjoyed a night of celebration, Job went before God and offered a sacrifice. He prayed and asked God to forgive them and cleanse them because he feared they might have sinned. He was a priest to his family. But it is more clearly set forth in the Levitical priesthood as shown in Exodus, Leviticus and Numbers in the Old Testament, and is set forth in perfection in Jesus Christ, our Lord.

## The Need for a Priesthood Because of Man's Alienation from God

God ordains the idea of the priesthood, and therefore, it must be a need. The need for priesthood arises from man's alienation from God. This is an integral part of biblical truth, just as hydrogen is a part of water, and you cannot have water without hydrogen. Therefore, you cannot have Bible truth without the doctrine that man has broken with God in what the Bible calls "alienation" in the great Fall that took place in the garden of Eden.

Any religion that ignores the truth that man is fallen and separated from God is a sham religion. Fallen man has morally pulled away from God and separated himself from God's fellowship so that he is said to be without hope and without God in the world. This being the condition of man, somebody has to make reconciliation between God and man to bring them back together again. This is where the idea of the priesthood lies.

Granted that man desired to return to God, he could not return because sin is in the way. A moral breach has occurred, a violation of the laws of God. Man is a moral criminal before the bar of God. Until satisfaction is made, until this breach is healed, until justice is satisfied, man cannot return to God even if he wanted to. This is what the Bible teaches, and anything else is less than Bible doctrine. If I did not believe this, I would close my Bible and lecture on Wordsworth or Shakespeare.

I have noticed that in recent years a serious error has developed among religious people in general. I fear that its focus is on what I will call a Christ-less nature mysticism. This is even invading what is termed as the evangelical church. When the fall of the year comes around, these nature mystics imagine a little man with a paintbrush painting the leaves, and some get very watery eyed about this. Again, in the spring, when the frogs begin to make their music in the little ponds, man's thoughts turn to love and the kind of things the poets write about. That is very dangerous, because if it is cross-less—without redemption, without Christ and without a proper reconciliation—it can be deadly. Yet, there are churches spending millions of dollars on fabulous buildings, but the congregation never hears a thing, year in and year out, about reconciliation.

Today's church faces the danger of a cross-less Christianity. A preacher will get up in front of the congregation and talk so piously about the "Great All Father." Or he might say, "This we ask in the spirit of Jesus." He did not ask it in the name of Jesus, but in the spirit of Jesus. He was a nice fellow, not wanting to offend anybody and surely too nice to embrace the cross.

This does not represent the biblical focus of Christianity. We must get back to the idea of a priesthood. We must get back to the idea of God on one side and man on the other, and the two of them alienated from each other. This alienation is not by the fault of God, but by the fault of man. We must get back to a sacrifice and a priest who can come between God, who is holy, and man, who is unholy, and bring the two of them together. That is priesthood.

## Priestly Qualifications

The Scripture tells us that a priest had to have several qualifications. First, the priest had to be ordained of God. "And no man taketh this honour unto himself, but he that is called of God, as was Aaron" (Heb. 5:4). Nobody could come out of the bush and say, "I'm a priest." God had to ordain the man or else he was a false priest. All the false priests around the world are self-ordained men. But there had to be a priest in Old Testament times that God ordained.

Then he had to be ordained "for men." God appointed the priest to help men. God needs no help, and no priest can give God any help. It is man that needs help, and the work of the priest was to atone for man's sins. The formula was given in the book of Leviticus, the fifth chapter, where it says: "And he shall sprinkle of the blood of the sin offering upon the side of the altar; and the rest of the blood shall be wrung out at the bottom of the altar: it is a sin offering. And he shall offer the second for a burnt offering, according to the manner: and the priest shall make an atonement for him for his sin which he hath sinned, and it shall be forgiven him" (Lev. 5:9-10).

There is the idea of the priesthood. It was an offering made for man to God by the priest. The priest was to represent God to man and man to God. Before God, he pleads for the man he represents. He instructs. He exhorts. With complete sympathy and understanding, he goes to God for man. This he can do because he himself is a man.

But the breakdown in the Old Testament was that the priest, when he went before God, to stand between a holy God and fallen man, was embarrassed, because he had to atone not only for the sins of the people he was reconciling, but he had to atone for his own sins as well. This was where the breakdown was. This was why Isaac Watts could write in his hymn "Not All the Blood of Beasts":

> Not all the blood of beasts
> On Jewish altars slain
> Could give the guilty conscience peace
> Or wash away the stain.
>
> But Christ, the heavenly Lamb,
> Takes all our sins away;
> A sacrifice of nobler name
> And richer blood than they.

The priest could not, by the blood of the sacrifice he made, take sin away completely, but only partly. God forgave sin and covered it until the time when Christ, the Great High Priest, came. When Christ came, He qualified completely as the one who could reconcile God and man. He was ordained of God.

That was qualification number one. "Thou art my son. Thou art a priest forever." He wanted reconciliation for the people. He had compassion. Christ qualified as the priest, and He became the author, the source and the giver of eternal salvation.

## Trust and Obey

There is a simple song in our hymnal called "Trust and Obey," by John Henry Sammis, that expresses something very fundamental:

> Trust and obey, for there's no other way
> To be happy in Jesus, but to trust and obey.

I believe that "trust" and "obey" are two wings of a bird. A wise old writer once wrote, "Two wings of a dove don't weigh her down." She rises by means of them. "Trust" and "obey" are the two wings of the Christian. We trust and we obey. We obey because we trust. We trust in order that we might obey. If we try to obey without faith, we get nowhere. If we try to have faith without obedience, it ends in nothing.

Christ has given eternal salvation to those who obey Him and to them who believe Him, for obviously the two are synonymous, if not identical. They are like two sides of a coin. I cannot split that coin edgewise with a fine saw and then try to buy anything with it. The salesperson would see one side of it and think it is all right, but when he took it in his hand, he would say, "What did you do? What's the matter here? That's only half a coin." And he would toss it back to me. You cannot pass one side of a coin. It takes two sides.

Trust is on one side of the coin, and obey is on the other. But the Church has taken a fine saw and split them, saying, "You don't have to obey. Just believe." Everything is "believe." You cannot divide that coin. You cannot separate it; if you do, it is no good. It is not just trust; it is not just obey. It is trust and obey. Believe God and then go get obedience. You will find that it will become in your heart eternal salvation. Jesus Christ will become your all in all.

Some try to find their own way or perhaps a shortcut. But there are no shortcuts on the pathway to God's presence. Moses spent 40 years on the backside of the desert before he came to the burning bush. I am quite sure that for Moses, who had grown up in Pharaoh's court, those 40 years were anything but convenient. God's timing, however, is always perfect; therefore, only He can be our guide. Only He can direct us in this path into the presence of God.

The pathway into God's presence has nothing to do with convenience or shortcuts. We have a Great High Priest who did not take a shortcut but rather went all the way to the cross, and now He is seated on the right hand of God the Father. He went the full distance to become our Mediator and High Priest.

What if Christ would have taken a shortcut to the cross? Remember that night, that very dark night in Gethsemane, when Jesus prayed, "O my Father, if it be possible, let this cup pass from me: nevertheless not as I will, but as thou wilt" (Matt. 26:39). Jesus took no road of convenience, nor did He seek a shortcut. He is our guide because He prayed, "Not as I will, but as thou wilt." He earned our trust and our obedience because He did not take the path of convenience but went the way of the cross and died for us and became Our Great High Priest.

Jesus Christ, the great High Priest ordained of God and ordained for man, is the only guide to usher us into the presence of God. This may be the reason the enemy of man's soul strives to come between God and us. But those who have found Christ have found the perfect Guide, and in following Him have found that rest and peace are in God's presence.

## That I Might Know Him
### by Max I. Reich (1863–1945)

That I might know Him! Let this be life's aim,
Still to explore the wealth stored in His Name.
With heaven-bought intelligence to trace
The glories that light up His sinless face:
That I might know His power day by day,
Protecting, guiding in the upward way:
That I might know His Presence, calm and pure,
Changeless midst changes, and midst losses sure:
To dwell with Him, in spirit, day and night;
To walk with Him by faith, if not by sight;
To work with Him, as He shall plan, not I:
To cleave to Him, and let the world go by:
To live on earth a life of selfless love;
To set the mind and heart on things above:
Till I shall see Him without vision dim,
And know Him as I know I'm known of Him.

# 5

# Man's Revolt Against God's Presence

*Now of the things which we have spoken this is the sum:*
*We have such an high priest, who is set on the right hand of the*
*throne of the Majesty in the heavens.*

Hebrews 8:1

Certain things are fundamental to human morality. That is, wherever you find man you will find a basic agreement on certain aspects we call morality—honesty, courtesy, neighborliness. Although humanity is sliding down a slippery slope, there are still things, from the human standpoint, that are considered moral—not necessarily things that God can approve as moral, but things that are common among humanity.

Perhaps the most basic agreement that can unite us is the idea that God exists and that He is the sovereign Majesty in the heavens. Along with that basic belief is the belief that we must go back again to God for the final judgment for the deeds done in the body. An old hymn by Charles Wesley, "A Charge to Keep I Have," reminds us of this:

A charge to keep I have,
a God to glorify,
a never-dying soul to save,
and fit it for the sky.

In Ecclesiastes we read, "Let us hear the conclusion of the whole matter: Fear God, and keep his commandments: for this is the whole duty of man. For God shall bring every work into judgment, with every secret thing, whether it be good, or whether it be evil" (Eccles. 12:13-14). There is a lot of difference between the man who is convinced that this is true and the man who doubts it or does not believe it at all. For if we believe that we must fear God, that this is our whole duty and that God shall bring every work into judgment, whether it is good or evil, there is going to be a difference in the way we view God's moral law.

## Majesty in the Heavens

Human morality rests upon this belief: There is a Majesty in the heavens. I believe also that human decency is fundamental. And human decency depends upon an adequate conception of God and of human nature. Accordingly, the atheist could not possibly have an adequate view of human nature. Any view that excludes the possibility that we come from God and that we shall return to God will have a detrimental effect upon human morality.

So we have faith in God, and we build on this rock. Saint Patrick himself prayed that prayer every day:

I arise today
Through a mighty strength, the invocation of the
Trinity,
Through belief in the threeness,
Through confession of the oneness
Of the Creator of Creation.[1]

I believe that when we arise in the morning, it ought to be in a mighty strength, believing in God the Father Almighty, maker of heaven and earth.

## Throne and a Kingdom

The Bible teaches that creation is a universe. That is, all that we see about us, from the farthest star that can be picked out by the most powerful telescope down to the tiniest cell seen through a microscope, and all things living and inorganic that make up what we call the world, this is a universe. It is one vast, single system embracing matter in spirit and life and mind and time and space, and all beings that are in it. The Bible teaches that these are not separated—they are not independent of each other—but are united and working harmoniously.

According to medical research, cancer is simply a condition in which cells no longer take orders from the rest of the body. A cancer is composed of free cells, anarchic cells; they are not subject to the balance and order of the rest of the cells of the body. They go wild, and soon they have brought the victim to death. If everything in the world were independent of everything else, you would have a universal cancer throughout the vast universe. So God brings everything together, interlocks them and makes them interdependent.

A stone could not be moved on the seashore but it would change in some manner the balance of the world. A leaf could not fall from a tree but it changes the order of nature a little bit . . . just that much. There is not a baby born into the world but makes the world a little different. The man or woman who dies and goes out of the world changes the world just a little bit, for all things interlock and depend upon each other.

The Bible further teaches that this universe, this "uni" (meaning "one"), this one great interlocking system has a central control. And that control is called the throne of God. The universe is controlled from that center. This seems logical to me. You know what would happen to the human body if it had no central control? There have been many fables and stories made up and told about the body that would not obey the head, and you can imagine what it would be like. There must be a head on every organism or else there could be no harmony, no coordination, no cooperation, no life.

Every organization has to have a head. If you organize anything, even a simple literary guild consisting of half a dozen women, they will always have a president. And the president must preside. It goes right on up to the largest empire that ever touched the world. Right on up to the great nations of the world. Every organization must have a head. That is logical.

So, if any organism has to have a head, if a machine has to have a head, an organization has to have a head, is it not logical to believe that somewhere in this vast universe, there is a throne where somebody runs it? I believe that is true. And I believe that the one on the throne is God, the Majesty in the heavens. The Bible refers to this center of control as the throne of God. And from that throne, God governs His universe according to an eternal purpose. That eternal purpose embraces all things. "All things" are two little words used often in the Scriptures, yet they are bigger than the sky above. They are bigger than the entire world. They are big because they take in all things.

So, we have the Majesty in the heavens, sitting upon His throne. Then someone is sitting on the right hand of that throne. Why? And who is He? He is Jesus Christ, the minister of the sanctuary, which God made, not man. The reason for His being there, in brief, is this: A province revolted in what we call the universe. In all this interrelated, interdependent, interlocking universe, one province revolted and said, "We don't want to be ruled by the head. We will not be ruled from the throne. We will rule ourselves. We will build this great Babylon up to heaven. We will not have God rule over us." That province we call "mankind." And mankind inhabits the little rolling sphere we call "the earth."

Some inquire if man exists anywhere else in the universe, and astronauts go up to find out. I do not think he exists elsewhere, because the Scripture says the earth has been given to the sons of men. I think the earth belongs to man. They have not done much with it, and they have not done a very good job, but it belongs to the sons of men.

That province is now in revolt against the Majesty of the heavens. What is God going to do? God could, with a wave of His hand, sweep that province out of existence. But what did He do? God sent His only begotten Son that He might redeem that province and bring it back into the sphere of the throne again, back into the sphere of the Kingdom. And that Kingdom is called "the kingdom of God." When a man is converted, he is born again into the kingdom of God. What does that mean? It means that he is born out of the old rebellious province into a new Kingdom, and admits that there is a throne, which he did not admit before.

No sinner admits to the throne of God as being valid and the right of God to rule over him. He can talk about God, and he will appeal to God, and he will use the name of God, but he will not obey God. That is why he is what he is. That is why he is a sinner and why he is called a sinner. That is why it is said that he will perish unless he repents and is born again. When he repents and is born again, he leaves the old world, the old province that revolted, and moves into the kingdom of God and comes under the rulership of the triune God again. That is how simple it all is.

You cannot get there by being baptized, though we all ought to be baptized, according to the teaching of Jesus. We do not get there by joining a church, although we all ought to join a church. You do not get there by praying; you can pray to the end of your life, 24 hours a day, and not get there. It is coming into the Kingdom by an act of the will, through Jesus Christ the Lord, that gets me out of the old, revolted province and into the kingdom of God and under the rule of the throne of God again.

## The One Who Returns Us to the Kingdom

God became man in order to rescue sinful man. This He did by forfeiting His own life that He might bring back to God again

70

those who had revolted. This, Jesus Christ our Lord did, and now we have Him sitting on the right hand of the throne of the Majesty in the heavens.

We have Christianity now intermixing everywhere, and everybody trying to do a little bit of good. But the essence of Christianity is this:

> Ye men of Israel, hear these words; Jesus of Nazareth, a man approved of God among you by miracles and wonders and signs, which God did by him in the midst of you, as ye yourselves also know: Him, being delivered by the determinate counsel and foreknowledge of God, ye have taken, and by wicked hands have crucified and slain: Whom God hath raised up, having loosed the pains of death: because it was not possible that he should be holden of it (Acts 2:22-24).

And, of course, "This Jesus hath God raised up, whereof we all are witnesses. Therefore being by the right hand of God exalted, and having received of the Father the promise of the Holy Ghost, he hath shed forth this, which ye now see and hear" (Acts 2:32-33).

There is a throne. And the one who sits on the throne is one of us—Jesus Christ—and the world has revolted against that throne. Christianity says to the world that they can come back to the throne through Jesus Christ the Lord.

This is what excited and thrilled the Early Church. They were not excited about the politico-industrial questions that excite so many religious leaders today. Everybody seems to jump on the political bandwagon, believing that it is the church's obligation to control government. But in the Early Church, those men and women baptized with the Holy Ghost, as recorded in the second chapter of Acts, were excited about other things.

They were excited about God on the throne. They were thrilled about Christ on the right hand of God the Father and His coming again in clouds of glory. They talked about the consummation of all things, the downfall of iniquity, the purgation of the world, the cleansing of the starry heavens above. They were intoxicated with thoughts about the glorified Christ who would soon return.

Above all things, they talked about that man who sat on the throne. "This man whom you crucified," they said, "He is at God's hand, alive forevermore and He is one of us." And they went out ablaze with that. These converted people, these disciples said, "Did you know that one of us is in a position equal to God, next to God in power and authority with all power given unto Him in heaven and in earth?" (see Acts 4:10-12). They went everywhere telling that this God was the man Jesus, and that one of our number had been exalted to deity.

## The God-Man Question

I read once of a man explaining that Christ was man but not a man. I wonder how that could possibly be. How could a thing be a "horse" but not a "horse"? Do you ever see "horse nature" floating around somewhere like a glutinous, ill-formed mass of cloud? Human nature can only be where a human being is. So instead of saying Christ is man but not a man, we must say that Christ is a man. "For there is one God, and one mediator between God and men, the man Christ Jesus" (1 Tim. 2:5). Jesus is a man, He is at God's right hand and He sits on the throne.

Therefore, we worship this man as God. We worship no other man, but we worship this man as God. And this man was believed to be God by the Early Church, and they worshiped Him as God. They said, "Now this man here, Jesus, is God." Then, of course, as they began to refine it metaphysically, people said, "But He's a human being, and how can you get on your knees to a human being? That would be idolatry." The New Testament Christians said, "This human being is different. He has union with the eternal Godhead, so that when you're worshiping Him, you're not worshiping idolatrously; you're worshiping God."

After they had gone on joyously worshiping for a century or two, the old theologians thought out a name for it. They called it the "hypostatic union." And because they had found a name, they thought they had explained it.

## Hypostatic Union

If you saw a strange-looking creature with feathers in front and hair behind and two tails and three horns and it was an odd-looking thing that was part duck, and somewhat like a cat, and it was waddling about, you would have all the scientists confess that they never saw anything like it. And then some scientist comes along with a name for it. And so he names it, and everybody says, "Now we know what it is." No, you do not. You just named it; that is all.

So it is with the hypostatic union. The question was, "How can God and man be one?" Nobody knew how, so they called it the hypostatic union, which means that the substance of God and the substance of man are united in one, so that when you are worshiping that man Jesus, you are worshiping God. That has satisfied everybody ever since, except the liberals, and you cannot satisfy them anyway.

I heard another name for it that I also like. I think this is a good one, maybe better than the "hypostatic union." They call it a "Theanthropic Conjoinment."

"Theanthropic" is such a beautiful little word. "Theo" is God, and "thrope" is man. Therefore, you have man and God in conjoinment. God and man united. Although I still do not understand it, I can kneel before Him and cry, "My Lord and my God," for there is a man at the right hand of God.

If we could look into heaven now, we would be introduced to creatures that would exhaust all human explanation. There would be six-winged creatures when two wings were all we were used to. And we would see creatures with wheels in the middle of wheels, coming out of the fire. We would see broad-winged angels and seraphims that burn. We would see strange creatures, and we would not understand them. All of these things would defy everything that man knows this side of glory.

Then somebody would say, "Now, wait! Look there. I see something that looks like the form of a man." Sure enough, you would recognize Him. It would be Jesus. He would be one of us. Moreover, we would step up to Him and say, "We're brothers. I know you. You're of my race. You belong to me."

Don't you feel good, for example, when you're traveling in South America or Germany or Asia, and a fellow walks up to you, and you look at each other and he speaks, and you say, "You're an American." He replies, "Yeah. I'm an American. I live in Chicago." You smile. In the little traveling I have done around the world, I cannot get over wanting to turn a flip-flop handspring backward when I see the American flag or when I see somebody that I know is an old Yankee. I like them not because they are any better, but there is something in you that knows your own people.

Suppose that I were wandering through heaven and saw an archangel but could not speak his language. Suppose that I saw a cherubim and could not speak his language, or a seraphim. I would be bashful around him. I would say he burns . . . I cannot go near him. Then, suddenly, I see a man. I would say, "Wait! Don't I know you?"

"Yes, I'm Jesus, whom you crucified, whom God raised from the dead. And I am here for you, pleading your cause before the Father's throne."

There before the throne is the man, Jesus Christ the Lord. Not the victorious God, which would have been no news to herald to the world. The good news is not that God is victorious. How could the sovereign Lord God be anything else but victorious? But what the Early Church said was there is a man victorious, a man who is joined to God, and that man is victorious, and we are blessed in Him. And so if we are in Him, we can be victorious too.

## Reunited with God in Christ Jesus

I think that we are living on the very outskirts, the far margin of the kingdom of God. We are in it, but we are just barely inside the door. Christians ought to recognize that our nature has been joined to God's nature in the mystery of the Incarnation.

75

And when Christ died on the cross and rose again, and began to join individual Christians to His body, He meant that we were to have the same victory He had. He meant that we were to have the same high privilege He had at God's right hand. He said, "I in them, and thou in me, that they may be made perfect in one; and that the world may know that thou hast sent me, and hast loved them, as thou hast loved me" (John 17:23).

One of the primary missions of our Lord was to convey to unbelieving people that they occupy the same place as He does in the heart of God. We are there because of the absolute worthiness of the Lord Jesus Christ who is our head. He is the representative of us before God. And as the sample man, He is showing what kind of man He can make. He is the model man after which you and I are patterned. That is why the Lord will not let you alone.

We get used to a little viewpoint. We look at the world and at God and the kingdom of heaven from one tiny, dim crack. It is a crevice that we are peeking through, forgetting that if we would only dare to rise and have faith, that man at the right hand of God, sitting at the right hand of the throne, belongs to us and we belong to Him, and whatever He is, we can be in Him. I tell you, it might change our whole lives. But here we are, the same as before.

I do not believe in change for change's sake. I recommend that we raise our eyes to God, the Majesty in the heavens, and that we look long and hard and reverently at Him in faith, and see at His right hand one of us, and say, "If he can be there, I can be there. If He is accepted of God, I am accepted in Him, in the Beloved. If God loves Him, He loves me. If He is safe, I am safe. And if He has conquered, I can conquer. And if He's victorious, I can be victorious."

Some morning, get up and allow the power of God to come on you, and allow Him to bless you. It would be quite a different change from what you used to be. Nevertheless, it would be wonderful. Why not let us seek the faith of God in Jesus Christ? Never go to God as some poet of paganism might go: from the outside. Always remember, "No man cometh unto the Father, but by me" (John 14:6). Any man can come unto the Father by Him.

So let us come. Let us practice it. Begin now. Let us move into the heart of God and live in that heart of God victoriously.

Of all the things I have been saying, this is the sum: We have a great high priest who has sat down at the right hand of the Majesty of the throne, of the Majesty in the heaven, being a minister of the sanctuary, which God built, and not man.

From our human point of view, man has always revolted against the presence of God, starting in the Garden of Eden. The first Adam took us away from the presence of God, while the second Adam, Christ, leads us straight into God's presence. The revolt of man is overturned by the redemptive action from the throne on high. God has paved the way into His presence and never winces in the face of man's revolt.

## Now to the Lord a Noble Song
### by Isaac Watts (1674–1748)

Now to the Lord a noble song!
Awake, my soul, awake, my tongue,
Hosanna to the eternal name,
And all his boundless love proclaim.

See where it shines in Jesus' face,—
The brightest image of his grace;
God, in the person of his Son,
Has all his mightiest works outdone.

Grace! 'Tis a sweet, a charming theme;
My thoughts rejoice at Jesus' name;
Ye angels, dwell upon the sound;
Ye heavens, reflect it to the ground.

Oh, may I reach the happy place,
Where he unveils his lovely face,
His beauties there may I behold,
And sing his name to harps of gold.

**Note**
1.  From *The Lorica (The Deer's Cry)*, Breastplate of St. Patrick, A.D. 433.

# 6

# THE NATURE OF GOD'S PRESENCE AMONG MEN

*We have such an high priest . . . a minister of
the sanctuary, and of the true tabernacle, which the
Lord pitched, and not man.*

HEBREWS 8:1-2

In order to comprehend the nature of God's presence among us, we must explore two aspects: the transcendental and the mystical. That is, there are certain concepts that are necessary to the Christian faith. The Word of God interlocks so completely that if you destroy any one part of it, you destroy the rest. That is why I have no place in my heart or in my head for a liberal, because a liberal insists on believing what he wants to believe, even rejecting what does not suit him. The result is that he has destroyed everything, because each thing depends upon everything else.

## God's Transcendence

The very nature of God's presence transcends human nature and is therefore beyond the grasp of mere human thought. When we come to the Scriptures, we must remember that all the way through the Bible, we are taught what sometimes has come to be called the "transcendental view of the world." The word "transcendental" means a dozen things in philosophy. But what I mean by it is that somewhere there is an absolute. Somewhere there is that which is not relative; it is fixed and final and can have no beginning and no ending. It transcends life, time, space, matter, motion, law and all these things, and we call that one, God. When Christians talk about Him, we call Him "our Father, which art in heaven."

That is one of the great truths of the New Testament, which if removed, you have done to the Scripture what you do to a sweater when it unravels. If you take a thread and just pull it along enough until you have pulled it out into one long thread, you have destroyed the sweater. Likewise, if you attempt to pull out this great, simple truth that God is God and that He had no beginning and that He created all things "that are in heaven, and that are in earth, visible and invisible, whether they be thrones, or dominions, or principalities, or powers: all things were created by him, and for him" (Col. 1:16), you unravel the sleeve of Christianity until you have got nothing left but a memory. It is essential to accept this truth.

I know that many people do not accept it. Liberals deny it and the materialists and certain scientists, but we do not care what people deny. Our job in life is not to deny, but to affirm. And regardless of how it sounds to some, we affirm that there is another world above this world, of which this world is but the shadow; and in that world there is a throne, and on that throne there is a God ruling His universe.

## The Mystical Element

Recognizing this transcendence is a mystical thing. By the word "mystical," I mean nothing of the esoteric religion of the East. I mean that there is such a thing as a Christian knowing God and meeting God for himself. That we can press our way into the sanctuary of the holy of holies, and with our hearts, we can meet, know, feel, sense and experience God in a manner more wonderful than any man or woman can experience any human thing or any human being. This is what is taught here, and this is basic to Christianity.

To deny the presence and existence of a transcendental world of which God is the head and the creator and the Lord, and to deny the mystical element of Christianity, you might as well close your Bible and go for a walk, because you will never understand it. If Christianity is reduced to a doctrine that can be explained with no intuitive knowledge, no direct knowledge of the heart of God, then where is the wonder of it? I would not give a dime to support a teaching that denied the presence of God in His universe and the fact that the human heart can know God through Jesus Christ.

## A Shadow of Heaven

Earth is a shadow of heaven—sin excepted, of course. Heaven shines downward and throws its shadows; and those shadows we call the earth and the things therein.

Wherever sin is found, however, it is a shadow of hell and never can be of heaven. Sin is a disease, a deformity, a plague, a blight, a treason, a rebellion, an error, a sacrilege and a perversion. It is all of those things and so it can be no part of heaven, for there is nothing of heaven in it and nothing in heaven like it. Sin is a sinister presence in the universe, which God has permitted to be here for a little while. Its days are limited and numbered by the determinate counsel and foreknowledge of God

When His good pleasure comes, He is going to destroy sin from the universe and beat it and chase it out of His universe until there is no sin left. So earth is the shadow of heaven.

## Oneness Between Heaven and Earth

Genesis 1:1 tells us, "In the beginning, God created the heaven and the earth." The universe is one—one Creator, one universe. God made the universe, and He did not make it in everlasting contradiction to itself. He made it as one. He did not make several parts of the universe opposed to each other but working harmoniously together. Christ, when He was on earth, taught the unity of heaven and earth and held that everything had its spiritual counterpart. For that reason, He was as much at home on earth as He had been in heaven.

There is a great deal of unnecessary mourning about our Lord coming down to the earth. A great many unnecessary and lugubrious tears are shed over our Lord's incarnation. Our Lord could become incarnated in the form of a man without embarrassment and without difficulty because when God made man in the first place, He made Him in His own image. It was a simple matter for the God who made the image to move into the image, so that the incarnation of Christ is not a great difficulty to believe at all. It is a mystery of godliness, but it is not hard to believe, though it is certainly impossible to understand.

Christ could be incarnated in the form of a man, but not in the form of an angel. No matter how high in the order of beings the angels may be, they were never said to be created in the image of God. Man is created in the image of God, and therefore, when God came down to be incarnated, He fit into the nature of man as neatly as a man's hand fits into a glove. And Jesus our Lord walked among men—among flowers and trees and babies and women and men and horses and all these things—just as naturally as He walked in heaven before He was incarnated, because heaven and earth, in the sight of God, are one.

The only thing that separates for the moment is that sinister presence we call sin—just as a healthy man may be suddenly very ill, and all that prevents him from being a healthy man is the presence of certain microbes or bacteria or virus in his veins. So in the universe, heaven and earth are one. But what is present in the world now is that virus we call sin. And by the blood of Jesus Christ and the power of His spirit, when that is purged away from the world, it will be seen that heaven can shine down on the earth, because God made both.

Jesus walked among men and talked about the birds and showed how the very birds could preach a sermon that we all ought to listen to. He talked about the flowers and pointed to the lily that grew around there, and said, "That lily can teach you a lesson, for that lily grows in its beauty and there isn't a man in all Palestine, not even Solomon when he was arrayed in all of his splendor, could be as good looking as this flower. God made this flower and the flower had nothing to do with it. Therefore, we give God the glory, and you stop worrying about yourself. Because God made the flowers, the Lord will take care of you." And the wind, the water, the light, life, growth, reward, punishment and all these things He talked about on earth, showing that they were projections downward of Law that was old as God and had their origin at the throne of God.

I pray and hope that Christians might get away from the notion that earth is under a shadow far away in some deep, subterranean cave of God's universe. And somewhere far away, shining in celestial splendor, there is a city, but there is no connection between the two. The devil would like us to believe that, but I do not believe it for a minute.

I believe that the Christian whose heart is alive, alert and sensitive to the light of God can see the city that "hath foundations, whose builder and maker is God." Moreover, he does not have to go to heaven to see it. I do not mean he sees visions in the night, wakes his wife and says, "I just saw a vision." I have never gone much for that kind of thing. I never had a vision in my life. I never had a dream I could not explain by something I ate or something I had seen or did not do. I am trying to say that the Christian, who is inwardly alive and has the life of God in him, will find himself at home among men and at home in heaven because he belongs in both, just as Jesus did.

When Jesus Christ walked on the earth, He was in the bosom of the Father, and there was no contradiction between those two statements. When a Christian walks upon the earth and tells his unbelieving friend, "I live in the bosom of God," the unbelieving friend raises his eyebrow and shakes his head and makes a little signal as though there's something wrong with the Christian. But there is nothing wrong with the Christian at all. The Christian is simply telling the truth: He is walking the earth, but he is in the bosom of God nevertheless. He is in the kingdom of God. "Ye are in God and God is in you," said Paul.

The Bible and nature bear the same signature upon them, so that we can conclude that whoever made one, made the other. Look again briefly at how nature is. We look up above us on a clear night and we see the stars. When I was young, I tried counting them but soon gave up. It was a good thing, because scientists say they are innumerable. That is, there are too many to count. You look up and see a little white spot, you call it a star, but the scientists say it is not a star at all, but a galaxy—a collection of stars. How many stars? Nobody knows. We have to have telescopic instruments to know that there must be billions upon multiplied billions of them.

When David looked up at the stars, it struck him how little he was in comparison with the size of the world. David knelt before God and with his harp in his hand, sang himself a song to God: "When I consider thy heavens, the work of thy fingers, the moon and the stars, which thou hast ordained; what is man, that thou art mindful of him?" (Ps. 8:3-4).

## Unredeemed Man's Response
## to the Wonder of Creation

There is the wonder of God's creation, but along comes man and begins to study it and log it and weigh it and measure it and create sophisticated instruments to see it so that he can weigh it and measure it better. This is unredeemed man's response to the wonder of God's creation.

## Astronomy

Nobody was ever blessed by astronomy, but how many millions of farmers at night have walked across the meadow on their way home from the store in the little town away, and looked up at the stars, and in their heart, thanked God that they were alive and that He was alive and up there. Astronomy is what man has made out of the stars.

## Botany

It is the same with flowers. God put flowers everywhere. I believe that everything is here for a purpose, and that God, being a God of reason, had a reasonable purpose for everything. I believe He made flowers because He had some creatures down here made in His image, and He knew those creatures had an aesthetic sense. They had the ability to appreciate beauty. So instead of God putting flowers down here and making them ordinary, He made them so beautiful that they bring a gasp of delight when you see the first flowers in the spring. You look at a flower and you say, "That flower grew there without any help at all. It couldn't even help itself." And then, "Thank God, He that made the flowers will keep me."

A botanist comes along, breaks that thing down into petals, stamens and all the rest. Soon you have a big book that nobody likes. We call that botany, which is what you inflict upon young people in high school and college, making them swear quietly that they will never look at a flower again. Instead of having God's beautiful world studied with God's beautiful flowers, you have a big book with fine print in it, and some fellow boring into it at night, trying to catch up so he can pass his test.

That is what we have done to God's flowers. We have turned it into botany.

## Geology

Then there are the rocks and the hills and the entire beautiful world God made under His heavens. And we like to look at them. I grew up in the state of Pennsylvania, that cherry land that I know now that it is. I did not know it then; I was too close to it to appreciate it. When you grow up with something, you are not as likely to appreciate it so much as something you see later in life. And I saw all those hills and little streams running among those hills and pine-clad mountains pushing up against the sky. I saw all that. Those are rocks and hills, and they are beautiful. And along comes some fellow with a microscope and a little hammer. And he is a geologist. And he teaches geology. Therefore, instead of being amazed at the rocks and hills, we have geology.

## Zoology

Then there are the birds. You used to see the birds that came early in the springtime, laid their eggs, hatched, sang among the branches and went back south again when the bitter autumn winds began to blow and the brown discouraged leaves were flying all about. I enjoyed seeing the birds. I used to like to see the pigeons come, reel and light on the peak of the barn and coo and puff out their necks at each other. I enjoyed the birds. But you give a bird and a rabbit to a professor, and he turns it into zoology.

Nature is reduced to a system instead of enjoyed for itself. God gave Adam the Garden of Eden, the trees and the beauty, and said, "Here, it's yours. Help yourself, but just take care of it. It's yours." Then man sinned, and when Adam, if he ever got back to see it, came back, he had a book under his arm. All that beauty is reduced to systematic science.

## Man's Study of God

The same thing is done with the Scriptures. God gave us the Word of the Lord, a letter from home. We used to sing a little song by an unknown composer back in camp meeting days that went like this:

> I have letters from my father
> In my hand, in my hand.
> Written by my elder brother,
> They are grand, they are grand.

It was not good hymnology, but it was wonderful truth— that we have a letter from God in our hands. Put that in the hands of a professor with thick glasses, and in a very short time he would produce theology that nobody would read.

A student in a Christian college wrote to me once and said, "Will you please help me? Am I backsliding, or what is going wrong? I suppose theoretically that the study of theology would be the most thrilling, the most delightful, the most enjoyable thing in the world, because theology is the study of God and the ways of God. And I would assume that it ought to be a delight, but this professor makes it impossible. I can't even enjoy it. I don't want to hear it."

I wrote back and explained it the best I could, because I had been up against that, too, in my life. So we have the Bible—the letters from God to His people. Then we take it, reduce it and systematize it, and soon you need a good education to understand it at all. The Lord never meant that. His Word is meant for all of His children.

This continent was conquered and settled by people who had never been through more than grade school. A *McGuffey Reader* was about all the education they had. But they could read, and they did have Bible translations given to them by men who were scholars, and so they lived on those good translations and never even knew there was anything else.

Simplicity and childlikeness. God hid these things from the wise and prudent, and revealed them unto babes (see Matt. 11:25). I have met many an old woman dressed in her old-fashioned black, who had not had a dress that was up to date or the latest fad for 40 years. I have seen these little old women and they have quit living in the earth at all. Oh, they cooked, sewed, cleaned house and went to the store and all that, but they were not living here. They were walking far off the sidewalk, living with God all the time. They were not brilliant people, not educated people, but they looked out on God's truth and saw it as a child sees flowers. They looked at God's truth and saw it as David saw stars, and as Isaiah saw the mountains: direct, unmediated, unsophisticated, unspoiled.

## A Picture of the Mystical that We Can Understand

We have a pattern for this way of seeing in the Old Testament tabernacle, which illustrated the presence of God among men. God's presence descended from above to lift humanity above the elements of the earth. The Lord said there was a pattern given to Moses on the mount. But now there is in heaven a sanctuary—a true tabernacle. There is an altar, a mercy seat and a high priest. And He said if Jesus were on earth, He would not be a priest. He could not be a priest, because there were priests already here on the earth after the order of Levi. But He said, according to the Old Testament Scriptures themselves, there has come a priest who is above the Levitical priesthood, after the order of Melchizedek, and this Jesus is the one. And He said this Jesus has a more excellent ministry than Levi, who had the tabernacle.

If you will read the books of Leviticus and Exodus and become acquainted with them and see what they say, you will see how beautiful the tabernacle and the priesthood was. There is something utterly beautiful about that Old Testament tabernacle and Levitical order. It was spoiled and stained by blood everywhere, for sin had spoiled and stained the world, and it took blood to wash the world. So all through the Old Testament order, there was blood: blood of lambs and pigeons and goats. But it was all pointing to the Lamb of God who would come to take away the sin of the world.

This whole tabernacle has been lifted and is now in heaven, and we have a priest there forever who offered Himself as the Lamb to end the sacrifice of all lambs. We have an altar there—not the altar in Jerusalem, but the altar in heaven. We have the Lamb there to take the place of all the beasts that were slain on Jewish altars. And we have an altar of incense there where our Lord pleads, to take the place of that transient altar of incense in the old tabernacle in Judea. Jesus Christ is the true priest, and strictly, He is the only priest. In a secondary sense, all of His people are priests. But in a primary sense, there is only one priest, and that is Jesus Christ the Lord, the High Priest.

## No Longer Anything Between Man and God

What does all this mean to us? It means that this glorious remedy remains now. In Old Testament days, once a year the high priest came dressed in his resplendent robes, and with blood not his own he went in through a veil so sacred that it was only to move once a year, and he sprinkled blood on the mercy seat between the wings of the cherubim where glowed the fiery Shekinah. All that yearly blood sacrifice for sin was fulfilled when our Lord gave up the ghost and said, "It is finished," and died on a cross. And what is taught here is that Jesus Christ washed the heavens so there is nothing between man and God now, if man will believe it. By the blood of the Lamb, God washed the heavens so that there is a friendly heaven arching over us now.

Jesus said, "Come unto me, all ye that labour and are heavy laden, and I will give you rest" (Matt. 11:28). "And the Spirit and the bride say, Come. And let him that heareth say, Come. And let him that is athirst come. And whosoever will, let him take the water of life freely" (Rev. 22:17), says the last book of the Bible.

The blood of the Lamb has washed away the evil that kept us away from God. Now, whoever will come may come, regardless of how dark his stain or how far off he may be from God. Any prodigal is the same distance from God as any other prodigal.

We hear of rapists, murderers and all the rest. Yet that rapist who rapes and kills in the park in the dark of the night is no further off from God than that proud businessman surrounded by his adoring family, who reads Shakespeare and listens to Beethoven. All are sinners, and all have come short of the glory of God (see Rom. 3:23). We are all without hope and without God in the world. Yet there is hope in God, if we will believe.

The Scriptures tell us there is a way opened through a fountain in the House of David, a way open through the rending of His flesh. So the rapist in the park, though we shudder at the terrible act he has committed, can come home if he will come. And the man who is up and out, he can come too. The cultured sinner can come and the uncultured, base sinner can come. All can come, because heaven and earth are united. Jesus Christ has washed away the division, the difference. Now we can come to God. Sin is still loose in the universe like a virus in the body, and the world is sick, desperately sick. But Jesus is the physician of souls and He can cure us and bring us to Himself by His blood.

Our hope for this world and for the world to come is a High Priest, an altar, a temple, a tabernacle, a shrine and a Savior by the throne above. This we Christians have. What bothers me is how we can keep so quiet about it and why it is that we can take it so soberly, almost sadly. It would seem to me that we Christians ought to be the happiest people in all the wide world.

## Now Let Our Cheerful Eyes
### by Philip Doddridge (1702–1751)

Now let our cheerful eyes
Our great High Priest above,
And celebrate his constant care
And sympathizing love.

Though raised to heaven's exalted throne,
Where angels bow around,
And high o'er all the hosts of light,
With matchless honors crowned.

The names of all his saints he bears,
Deep graven on his heart;
Nor shall the meanest Christian say
That he hath lost his part.

So, gracious Saviour, on our breasts
May thy dear name be worn,
A sacred ornament and guard,
To endless ages borne.

# 7

# FINDING TRUE FREEDOM IN GOD'S PRESENCE

*For every high priest is ordained to offer gifts and sacrifices:*
*wherefore it is of necessity that this man have somewhat also*
*to offer. For if he were on earth, he should not be a priest,*
*seeing that there are priests that offer gifts according to the law:*
*Who serve unto the example and shadow of heavenly things,*
*as Moses was admonished of God when he was about to make the*
*tabernacle: for, See, saith he, that thou make all things according*
*to the pattern shewed to thee in the mount.*

HEBREWS 8:3-5

A new way of worship was being opened for Israel by blood. God instructed Moses to make the tabernacle after a divine pattern shown to him on the mount. God gave them the tabernacle with its altar of sacrifice made of brass where beasts were offered, and the altar of incense typifying prayer. Beyond that, in the holy of holies, was the Ark of the Covenant with its gold lid, called the mercy seat. And over that golden mercy seat were two cherubim with their wings outstretched toward each other. Between the wings of the cherubim burned the awful fire, the Shekinah.

Then there were priests, born priests and anointed to exercise their function as priests. They wore garments—all symbolic and typical of heavenly things. Above them, the high priest—typical of the great High Priest who was to come. It took a tremendous amount of labor to construct altars, and this mercy seat, and this Ark of the Covenant and these tables and the walls and the curtains.

All these had to be made, and Moses was not permitted to draw a single plan. Not one. In making the veils, not one man was allowed to draw the pattern. Moses might have been qualified, as he was an educated man, a genius in his own right. Living in Egypt, he saw beautiful buildings about the palace where he grew up as a boy, the supposed son of Pharaoh's daughter. I would be happy to live in a house Moses designed, with his ability and experience. However, God instructed Moses, "I want you to make this earthly tabernacle a reflection of the tabernacle above, so the light shining down from God upon this area will reflect back to what it sees will be your earthly tabernacle. This will be here only a little while. Shadows do not remain very long. The light continues, but the shadows go. I want you to make this, and do not dare improvise. Don't you take any liberties with the score. Don't tack on anything. Don't do it, Moses. Stay by the pattern shown to you on the mount, because if you fail Me in the making of this, then there will be an imperfect reflection of the shining glory above."

## God Explains the Plan

God warned Moses not to fluctuate from the pattern He gave him on the mountain. Moses had his instructions and did not have liberty to change or improve on the pattern. This springs out of a threefold presupposition.

## Redemption Is Wrought by God

Redemption is wrought by God and not by man. There is not any place in the head of a man or in the fingers of a man, however skilled or brilliant, for redemptive plans or purposes. God purposed redemption in Christ Jesus before the world began, and it does not need any editing on my part or on the part of any living man.

## True Religion Is Revealed by God

True religion is not discovered or conscripted by man. Christianity grows downward from heaven, not upward from the earth. It does not stand upon the earth. Its roots are in heaven, so that man has nothing to say here at all. True religion is revealed from above.

Man has constructed many religions throughout the world, and some are very beautiful and meaningful, but they are not redemptive religions. God said, "This true religion, which you are to enjoy, comes from heaven above and all you are to do now is simply let the light above shine down and reflect the glory that is above." And when you pull away the Old Testament's mirror, there is no more any reflection. That is gone, but the eternal world above remains.

## Salvation Is Received from God

There is a third presupposition: Salvation is received from God and not achieved by man. If man had achieved salvation even a little bit, say by 1 percent, then God would have said, "Moses, I'm giving you a 99 percent perfect blueprint. You can doodle a little and write in and improvise and put in anything you want to put in, because I allow you 1 percent." Rather, God said, "No, Moses. I give you a plan that is 100 percent from Jehovah, thy God, so don't take liberties with the pattern." Heaven will tell earth how to live. Remember that. Heaven speaks and it is for earth to listen. Heaven commands and it is only for earth to obey, not to ask questions. Heaven calls and it is for earth to answer. Heaven invites and it is for earth to respond to the invitation.

The New Testament Church has also been handed the pattern, consisting of things eternally true, revealed by God. Commandments laid down by God, eternally true, and true for all nations, for each single nation and for all persons and for each single person, and true under all conditions, and not relative. We have today what is called the relativity of morals. When you come to the things of God, open your Bible and put away this woozy idea of relativity, this floating standard of morals. When God speaks, let the world listen. "O earth, earth, earth, hear the word of the LORD" (Jer. 22:29).

## God's New Testament Pattern Was Shown on the Mount

The pattern God has given us is a mirror reflecting God's truth from above. These truths are not relative and floating; they are true beyond debate. However, in this day of the panel discussion, half a dozen people sit around and pool their ignorance.

Nobody knows anything about the topic, but they sit around and discuss it.

Our admonition is, do not doodle the plan. Do not improvise. Do not stick in a single board or plank. Do not put one thread into the garment of God. Do not dare lay one foundation or put one pillar upright except God tells you to do it. Do not deviate from the pattern given by God Himself.

The trend today is for preachers not to be so dogmatic. After all, so they say, there is another side to everything. But there is only one side to what God says—and that is God's side. We, therefore, dare not allow ourselves to take another side and begin debating. The Word of the Lord is not debatable. And the commandments of Christ are not there to be discussed by a panel. They are there to be obeyed in humility and tears, in the power of the Holy Ghost within us.

What God has revealed to us in His Word is built into the Christian faith. They are the threads God works into the holy garment. They represent the philosophy by which all men live. This is where true freedom lies—not making it up as you go along, but discovering the immutable decrees of God.

The Word of the Lord stands. Here it is. What are you going to do about it? "The word that I have spoken, the same shall judge him in the last day" (John 12:48). "These are My words," says God, "and let no man add anything to them lest he be cursed. And let no man take anything away." God's words are not for me to edit and tinker with, but to believe and obey.

We are committed to the Bible pattern, and no man has any authority to add anything to it. No man has any authority to subtract anything from it, to alter it in any way, to remold it nearer to his heart's desire. "Look that thou make them after their pattern" (Exod. 25:40).

Some people are afraid of this kind of teaching. They do not want to be confined, or fenced in. They feel that to hold any dogmatic view like that is to be narrow, tame and static. That is the devil's argument, because the answer to it all is that the misery in the world is the result of our not believing God's pattern.

All the miseries in the world come originally from the human race not following the pattern shown on the mount. God laid down a few certain rules for them and said, "If you want to live in the light of my face, live like this."

Of course, everybody thought they knew better. Eve thought she knew better than the rest, and the result is the mess we are in. There will not be a tear shed in the world today—around the whole wide globe—but what is the result of broken hearts. The effect is people thinking they know better than God about things, taking things out of God's hands and taking them into their own. If Adam and his people—his race—had obeyed the pattern on the mount and lived the way God told them to, there would be no Cold War and no hot war and no graveyards and no bereavement and no cancers and no tuberculosis and no murders.

There are two ways to be dumb. One is not to go to school at all and the other is to go too long. I think some of these people have been in school too long. For example, take a sardine—as long as my little finger—into the middle of the vast rolling Pacific and put him down. Just before you put him down, say to him, "Now, sardine, after you've roamed around the ocean awhile, you're going to have to hunt another ocean." How long would it take that sardine to stagnate? It would take him a million years, and he would not have found the borders of that vast, rolling, undulating sea.

God has given us this wonderful world with its high-peaked, snowcapped mountains, and arched over it the star-studded sky, and made the winds to blow through her valleys, and clothed her in green and decked her with flowers. And He hath said, "This is yours now. Everything you put your foot on belongs to you. I've given this to the sons of men."

The temptation is to get anxious and say, "Watch that you don't stagnate, brother." According to the experts, we do not use one-third of the brain we already have. We spend our time fooling around, and the result is that we are not developing the mighty pattern that is within our own nature. I am not going to stagnate because I do not go to the moon or somewhere else up there and float around. I am doing pretty well down here, thank you. If you come to know God, you can go on to know God, because we are not dealing with matter, space, time, law and motion. We are dealing with the eternal God who made both the visible and the invisible. Take all the creatures God ever made, from the holy watchers beside the throne to the amoeba in the sea, they could all search into God for millions of years and eternities to come and not have found or even touched the hem of His garment.

Let men out in the world stagnate, but Christians do not stagnate. We have God, the everlasting, self-renewing fountain that never gets stale. Our mistake, and the mistake we have made all down through history, is in thinking that we know better than God. God says, "See thou make it after the pattern," and we say, "Well, we'll partly do that. We're glad for the inspiration of the pattern, sure. It's wonderful to have the inspiration of the pattern. But we do not think that it is necessary to stay by the pattern. If we do, we'll stagnate."

If that is true, then the one that goes the farthest from the pattern ought to be the happiest and freest man. But you know it is not so. If it is true that keeping the Word of the Lord binds us and makes slaves out of us; and repudiating the Word of the Lord and breaking the commandments of Christ sets us free, then the man who is the farthest from God ought to be the freest man. But it is exactly the other way around. The man who is the farthest from God is the greatest slave. Look at the man who has gone the farthest and who is away from God. If the drug addict says, "Let's cast God's cords from me," he has been temporarily freed from the commandments of God, but he has a monkey on his back. He is now a slave to drugs or alcohol or whatever.

In the city of Chicago, there are beautiful parks. There was a beautiful park off Sixty-Seventh Street and North with a hedge all the way around it. A beautiful, carefully trimmed hedge went all the way down one street, down another and down another. Of course there were openings and gates where you could go in and enjoy the park. But they had to remove that hedge because young men hiding in the hedges jumped out and attacked women. To get rid of this hiding place for moral morons, they had to remove the hedge so they would not have a place to hide. There is an example of your free man. He laughs at the pattern shown in the mount, and the commandments of Christ mean nothing to him. He is free. He is following his own desires. He is an unsuppressed animal. However, do not let your daughter near him.

If it were true that Christians are slaves and that there was a great deal of bondage associated in obeying the command-ments of Christ, and in living in obedience to the faith of our fathers, then Christians should have shackles on their wrists. And the beatniks and the rest should be the freest people in the world. Exactly the opposite is true. We are free as birds, and the bearded beatnik with his feet up and espresso coffee between his brown unscrubbed teeth is a slave to the opinion of the beatnik crowd. He is a nonconformist, he says, but as a noncon-formist, he is slavishly conforming to his nonconformity.

## Free Indeed

The four Gospels, the book of Acts, Romans, the Corinthian epistles, Galatians, Thessalonians, the epistles of John and all the rest are the patterns shown us in the mount. "He that hath my commandments, and keepeth them, he it is that loveth me: and he that loveth me shall be loved of my Father, and I will love him, and will manifest myself to him. . . . If a man love me, he will keep my words: and my Father will love him, and we will come unto him, and make our abode with him" (John 14:21,23).

The man to whom God has come and in whose heart God dwells is a free man compared with the man who is trying to be free in his own right. The murderer, the drunkard, the drug addict and the suicide—they are free from the commandments of Christ, but they are slaves to the devil. The Christian, according to Paul and Christian experience, gets free from the bondage of Satan and becomes a happy servant of Jesus Christ the Lord. I know there are households where the servants are better off than many householders are. In the kingdom of God, the humblest servant that serves by the kitchen sink is a happier, freer man than the lord of the manor across the street if he is not a Christian.

## Follow the Pattern
## Shown on the Mount

I do not apologize for being a Christian. I once looked up to highly educated men and felt they were so learned that if ever I would find out what they knew, I could not believe the Bible at all. I had an itch in my head to find out what they knew to see if it would invalidate what I believed. Therefore, I did a little reading on my own and found out that nobody knows enough. Furthermore, I venture to say that nobody can ever know enough to invalidate one word of the Scriptures or prove wrong one single sentence from the book of God.

Be careful to follow the pattern shown on the mount; that is where true freedom is found. Listen to people and you will go wrong. Listen to editors and those who feel they must amend the Word of God, change the truth and modify it, and you will go wrong. You will come under bondage to yourself, to the world and to the devil. However, if you will go free, you will find that freedom lies in obedience to God's laws. Therefore, the Christian is free when he is obeying his Lord. He is the freest of all beings unless it would be the angels above.

The airplane that flies up yonder is obeying the law of gravitation and all kinds of aerodynamic laws. Sometime when I have nothing else to do as I ride on an airplane, I read the literature explaining about the various engines. I find out there is not a single part in all great planes that is accidental. It is all put there in obedience to a law, which God Almighty had given to the material world. When the law is broken, down plunges the machine into the mountain below or into the sea.

The keeping of the law makes us free; the breaking of the law makes us slaves. So it is with beauty. So it is with the stars in the heaven that shine above. If you obey the pattern shown in the mount, you will be free and happy and completely at rest and be able to develop all of the hidden potentials that lie within your own nature. But if you refuse, if you fail, or if you let the Word of God stay outside your knowledge, you will find yourself in inevitable bondage.

Regarding God's Word, let us love it and live in it and eat it and drink it and lie down on it and walk on it and stand on it and swear by it and live by it and rest in it. This is the book of God. "Look that thou make them after their pattern, which was shewed thee in the mount" (Exod. 25:40). Clean up your life. Bring it around to the harmony of God.

If Moses had found some of his workers and said, "What's that thing there?" and the worker responded, "I don't know. I was just improvising," Moses would have rebuked the worker, "Take that out and burn it. Stay by the pattern shown thee in the mount." If Moses, Paul, or some other biblical saint were alive today and came to our average church, they would find a great deal of just improvising on the part of people who ought to know better.

Let us determine to obey God and do what we are told to do. Let us have faith and believe it. Let us not make the mistake of mixing the two—of trying to believe what we should do and do what we should believe. There are things to do and there are things to believe.

An old saint was once asked, "Which is more important: prayer or the reading of the Word?" He thought for a moment and then responded, "Which is more important to the bird, the right wing or the left?" That is a question I want to pose: Which is more important to a Christian, believing or obeying? For the sparrow flying through the air, both wings are equally important. With only one it is almost impossible to fly. So, we must believe God's Word and we must obey it. By these two wings, a man will rise to God in faith and humble obedience to the Lord Himself.

The truest Christian is the freest Christian, and the gospel of Jesus Christ sets slaves free. However, you say, "My experience with Christians has not taught me that they are the ideal people you've described." The reason is that very few Christians are prepared to go with God all the way. They go part of the way and then improvise. They follow the Lord until things look a little sticky and then they say, "Well, there's no use to get radical about this and be a fanatic. I think I can reason this out myself." So, they have a panel discussion and decide what the Lord really should have said there. The result is, of course, lukewarmness, which God will spew out of His mouth.

Let us return to the Book. Or rather, let us go forward to the Book, for we lag so far behind it. Thank God for the Book. See that you do all things after the pattern shown on the mount. See that your faith conforms to God's revelation. See that your footsteps walk in God's path. If you do that, God will be an enemy to your enemies and an adversary to your adversaries. And God will look after you.

True and undiluted freedom finds itself in the presence of God. Following the pattern set for us in God's Word will bring us into God's presence where we will discover this freedom. Every generation seeks for something new, when really they are seeking for something "other." It is this presence of God that is the "other" each generation seeks and longs for, if only they knew it.

## Blessed Are the Sons of God
### by Joseph Humphreys (1720–?)

Blessed are the sons of God,
They are bought with Jesus' blood;
They are ransomed from the grave,
Life eternal they shall have;

With them numbered may we be,
Here, and in eternity.

They are justified by grace;
They enjoy a solid peace;
All their sins are washed away;
They shall stand in God's great day;
With them numbered may we be,
Here, and in eternity.

They have fellowship with God,
Through the Mediator's blood;
One with God, through Jesus one,
Glory is in them begun;
With them numbered may we be,
Here, and in eternity.

8

# PAVING THE WAY INTO GOD'S PRESENCE

*For this is the covenant that I will make with the house of Israel after those days, saith the Lord; I will put my laws into their mind, and write them in their hearts: and I will be to them a God, and they shall be to me a people: And they shall not teach every man his neighbour, and every man his brother, saying, Know the Lord: for all shall know me, from the least to the greatest. For I will be merciful to their unrighteousness, and their sins and their iniquities will I remember no more. In that he saith, A new covenant, he hath made the first old. Now that which decayeth and waxeth old is ready to vanish away.*

HEBREWS 8:10-13

God does nothing that necessitates a reversal of His actions, nor does He do anything to contradict Himself. God says explicitly of Himself, "For I am the LORD, I change not" (Mal. 3:6). In other word, everything God does is in complete harmony with everything God does.

Even in the world of nature we see examples of God's harmonious working. David understood this when he wrote, "The heavens declare the glory of God; and the firmament sheweth his handywork" (Ps. 19:1). God has put together this world of ours with great care, with each part relying upon another part.

Therefore, when we approach the subject of coming into the presence of God, we must understand that there is nothing insignificant associated with it. The importance of coming into God's presence is seen in the meticulous planning that He put into it. We will find harmony and consistency all along the way into God's presence.

The way into God's presence as recorded in the Old Testament was provisional until the time when the New Testament was revealed. The Old Testament instructions were something like the scaffolding that goes up when erecting a building. When the building is completed, the scaffolding is removed. The Old Testament law was the scaffolding that was provisional for the time until the New Testament revelation of Christ. When the anticipated new came, the old was no longer needed and was done away with.

In the Old Testament, we can start with Abraham's altar, move on to Moses' tabernacle in the wilderness and then Solomon's Temple in all of its magnificence. We can follow this progression with great delight, but we must realize it is but scaffolding preparing the way for something greater. The writer to the Hebrews tells us that Christ is that greater one.

Everything in the Old Testament moves us toward the prize, which is Christ, the fulfillment of every Old Testament promise. Each promise was a plank in the scaffolding, enabling God to bring us closer into His presence. And once the destination was reached, the scaffolding was no longer needed.

This backward look at the Old Testament covenant serves to heighten our appreciation of the New Testament revelation of Jesus Christ. And what a glorious revelation He is! To the question, "what hath God wrought?" we answer simply, Jesus Christ.

## What the Old Covenant Reveals

In order to appreciate what the new covenant means to us as believers, we need to examine carefully the old Covenant. When we do, we will discover several things about it.

Let me make it clear that by "the law," I am not referring only to the Ten Commandments. That certainly was part of it, but it was given as part of a more comprehensive law, which included sacrifice, the priesthood and the altars—with the blood and the lambs and the beast and the bulls and goats. When we talk about the law, all of this is included.

As good as the Old Testament law was, and it was just and good in the best definition of those words, it had a weakness. The weakness of the Old Testament law had to do with its location. And by that, I mean everything about the Old Testament law had to do with the exterior and never the interior. The Bible clearly teaches that a man's conduct and character spring from within him. "What cometh out of a man," Jesus said, is what matters.

The weakness of the Old Testament law was that it could not deal with the life motivations of any person. It dealt mainly with the words: "thou shalt not" and "thou shalt." History has proven that you cannot change a man by legislating his actions. Only conduct can be legislated, but this never gets inside the man to affect his motivation.

The old covenant was imperfect by the nature of it, temporary in its continuance and inadequate in its effect. In this sense, the old covenant pointed to something beyond itself.

## What the New Covenant Implants

Throughout the Old Testament, God promised to provide an inward moral bent to holiness. He promised a new covenant to permanently replace the temporary old one. And the writer of Hebrews argues, if you are going to get a new covenant, you make old and obsolete the old covenant.

What the old covenant could not do because of its weakness, the new covenant in Christ accomplished and continues to accomplish. What this new covenant does is implant into the heart of a man a new nature, impelling him to act righteously. No longer is his conduct directed by an exterior law but by the law of Christ within him. This was the promise buried deep within the old covenant. "But this shall be the covenant that I will make with the house of Israel; After those days, saith the LORD, I will put my law in their inward parts, and write it in their hearts; and will be their God, and they shall be my people" (Jer. 31:33). Therefore, there is something implanted in the heart of a man redeemed by the blood of Christ that impels him to do that which is right.

What I am talking about is the nature of the redeemed man. The Christian has instincts within not found in the unsaved man. I know that the words "nature" and "instinct" are in bad repute in some learned and extremely eggheaded circles. Although refusing to use such words, at least they are willing to say that there is something within a man, a "native" factor in behavior. That is, there is an intrinsic, internal factor in behavior in every person.

This is clearly illustrated for us out in the world of nature. Back on the farm, we used to raise chickens. My mother always had a large flock of chickens to produce eggs for us. She had what she called a "setting hen," and looked forward to the time when all the chicks hatched. I always noticed as soon as one of those little chicks hatched from its egg it began acting like a chicken. There was something within it causing it to behave in a certain way. No sooner were they out of their shell until they were out scratching in the dirt, even though they had never seen any chicken before them scratch. They scratched by some native factor leading them to do acts not dependent upon any previous experience. The mother hen did not teach the little chicks how to do that. It came to them naturally. They possessed the instinct of a chicken.

On the farm, my father raised hogs as well as chickens. And the interesting thing about those pigs is that when they were born, they acted like pigs and never like a chicken, even though they lived on the same farm. Both the chicken and the pig had in them what I will refer to as a "native factor" in behavior, making them act like themselves. A chicken will always act like a chicken, and a pig will always act like a pig.

It is this tendency to action that leads to an end. Whatever this is in animals, birds, fish, worms and all the rest, it is that unknown factor that impels every creature to act like itself.

I grant you that this behavior can be altered by pressure from the outside. Go to any circus in town and you will find animals acting contrary to their nature. You might see a little monkey in a suit with a red hat mimicking the mannerisms of a man. But he is still a monkey inside. You can alter him on the outside, but you can in no way remove that unknown factor within that impels him to act like himself. As soon as the little monkey gets by himself or with other monkeys, he will act like himself. Temporarily, outside forces can persuade animals to act like something else, but when left to themselves, they automatically revert to their nature.

Of course, this has implications in the church. The church is notorious in using outside pressure to make a sinner act like a Christian. You can teach almost anybody to do almost anything. Baptize him, confirm him and feed him the Lord's Supper regularly; instruct him in the faith, and after a while he begins to act like a Christian. He is not a Christian because there is not that inward factor impelling him to righteousness and true holiness. Outside pressure is making him conform and act like a Christian. However, when he is away from that pressure, he reverts to acting like himself—a sinner. His instinct is always toward sin.

To make this perfectly clear, let's look at two extremes. Take the first archangel in Isaac Watts's hymn "Eternal Power, Whose High Abode":

Thee while the first archangel sings,
He hides his face behind his wings,
And ranks of shining thrones around
Fall worshipping, and spread the ground.

Compare that first archangel over against that old devil, which is called the "Dragon" and "Satan." It would be difficult to find two creatures as far apart morally as these two. Both have an unknown factor within telling them to act like themselves. The archangel instinctively acts like an archangel, and Satan always acts like himself.

The only thing I can say in Satan's favor is that he always acts like himself. When he is deceiving, he is acting like the devil; he is acting like himself. Remember what Jesus said about certain Jews who were persecuting Him: "Ye are of your father the devil, and the lust of your father ye will do" (John 8:44).

When the archangel is acting like an archangel, he is not acting because he has been trained to do so. He is acting from the inside. Something within him makes him act like an archangel, and he does not resist. He desires to do it just like the little chick does not resist the temptation to scratch; it scratches because something inside of it is impelling it to scratch. So the archangel is not comparing himself with someone else and saying, "I've got to act like an archangel." He acts like an archangel because he is an archangel.

This brings up the old question the Church has debated from time immemorial. Does a sinner sin because he is a sinner, or is he a sinner because he sins? Well, both are correct. We can go round the theological circle until by the grace of God we break out of that and we are a sinner no longer. Therefore, the sinner is one who sins, but he sins because he has been a sinner. When he sins, he is simply acting like himself.

The crowning achievement of the New Testament is to implant in the heart of a believing man an unknown factor that impels him to act righteously and holy.

# Birth Trumps Training

The question I want you to consider is simply this: Which is more important, the birth or the training? I suggested what training can do and what it cannot do. And so the matter comes down to this: the nature we have is the one we were born with. Training can go so far, but birth, especially the new birth, establishes the true nature. And this is the difference between what I will call "denominational churchianity" and true Christianity. We are training people every week to be good church people. But when left to themselves, they will revert to their real nature and act like themselves. They have been trained to act like a good Christian on Sunday, but it is only an act. The rest of the week they act like themselves, naturally.

People sang the songs of Israel without being Israelites. And people today can sing the songs of the Church without being truly Christians. Because once the song is over the true nature within takes over.

You say, "What right have you, in this bigoted manner, to rule men out of the Church?" I do not have any right to do anything at all. But under the grace of God and by the authority granted me by the Lord Jesus Christ, I do have this commission: to draw the line between him that serveth God and him that serveth Him not. And I dare to stand and say in His name that unless a man is born again, he cannot enter the kingdom of God. And no amount of training or religious accent we put on will ever do.

Something has to change within for every person. We call it the new birth. We call it the regeneration. No matter what we call it, there has to be implanted in the human spirit that which impels righteous conduct. You need to be regenerated because you were generated wrong in the first place. That "unknown factor"—God calls it "My law." He said, "I will put my laws into their mind, and write them in their hearts: and I will be to them a God, and they shall be to me a people" (Heb. 8:10). That is where we get it. A Christian is one who has had the laws of God inscribed in his heart at the motivational center of his life. That is a Christian. Nothing else qualifies.

With this new birth, this regeneration, comes an instinct that does not need exterior pressure to act.

## Deliverance from the Wild Factor

In our church, we once had a carpenter newly converted to Christ. One day when he was on the job, pounding away, he missed the nail, hit his thumb and let out a yell; that old language that would have curled the hair of an archangel filled the air. He surprised everybody by not falling on his knees confessing his sin. He simply smiled and said, "Glory to God."

For some people it sounded a little confusing, but it is not at all. For my recently converted carpenter friend it suddenly occurred to him that his old way was gone. Sure, his swear words jumped to his lips, but they were simply a reflex. They were his old habit, and he had fallen into it for a second. God, however, knew he did not mean it. Instead of getting all bent out of shape, spiritually speaking, he praised God that he had been delivered from that old life. The reflex was there, but something deeper was replacing that. Sometimes it takes a while, but my carpenter friend knew there was a time in his life when he would have cursed a blue streak without any kind of thought behind it. Now things were different.

The new birth changes things within. Sometimes it takes a while for it all to work outward. The apostle Paul understood this perfectly when he wrote, "Work out your own salvation with fear and trembling" (Phil. 2:12). The essential purpose of the new birth is to defeat and destroy within the human heart the old nature, or the wild factor. Our deliverance from this wild factor is from within and not from merely trying to contain it and control it with outside pressure.

The New Testament teaches the presence of conflicting factors in the Christian's life. There are conflicting factors that sometimes overcome him: weakness of the flesh and the influence of the world; lust and old habits. In the seventh chapter of Romans is a classic way of a holy man who sometimes felt a factor stirring within him that impelled him to be unholy, and he cried, "O wretched man that I am! who shall deliver me from the body of this death?" (Rom. 7:24). He went on in the eighth chapter to show the provision made toward deliverance from these wild factors that lie in us, factors we call "the flesh" or "carnality" or "the old man." There are a dozen names given to this.

Thank God, we can have complete deliverance from the old nature and the old instincts and that old way of life. Behold, the new nature cometh!

## What Is of Man and What Is of God

In the book of Hebrews, we read, "And they shall not teach every man his neighbour, and every man his brother, saying, Know the Lord: for all shall know me, from the least to the greatest. For I will be merciful to their unrighteousness, and their sins and their iniquities will I remember no more" (Heb. 8:11-12). The question is, can religion be taught?

I want everybody to know that I certainly do believe in religious education, if we understand what is meant by it. I believe it is important that doctrine and ethics be taught. I think our children should be taught in the Sunday School the things of God—the Scripture and what the Bible teaches. All of this is good and should be done. Our children need to be taught what the Bible says about "Obey your parents, do not lie, and do not steal." There are many things that we can be teaching our children.

But the serious error facing the church today is its belief that salvation can be taught. Set a person down or a group of people and teach them what the Bible says and ask them if they believe it and if they accept it and so forth. When everybody nods their head in the affirmative, we lead them into believing that they have now been born again.

What we must teach is that salvation happens in a man's life because he believes that doctrine that he has heard. Anybody can pass a test and recite the catechism from the first or the last, letter perfect, and still not be a Christian. It is impossible to make a person a Christian by teaching. However, you can compel him to want to be a Christian. You can show him how to be a Christian. And when he has become a Christian, you can teach him, as Jesus said, "These things have I spoken unto you" (John 14:25). But you cannot make him a Christian by teaching him.

Life cannot be created by the act of teaching. Nobody yet has ever come up with the curriculum that could bring a baby into the world. Babies are born out of life. But after that baby is born, you can begin teaching him and eventually send him away to college, and he can learn what he needs to learn. But the crucial thing is that you have to start with life.

What I often ponder is how many Christians are there who are Christians only by instruction, religious education or having somebody manipulate them by dunking them in a baptismal pool or sprinkling water on them?

How many of these people come to church every Sunday, take part in the services on Sunday and yet are not known for being Christians, because away from the church they do not act like a Christian? They are Christians by assumption, by manipulation or instruction, rather than by regeneration.

Salvation implants within the human heart an unknown factor in helping that person to holiness. The true Christian cries out to the Father by impulse of the Holy Spirit and does not ask to be taught. Nobody says to this new Christian, "Repeat after me, 'Abba Father'." He says "Abba Father" because the Spirit of the Son, in his heart, is telling him to say it.

Here is where we need to understand what is of man and what is truly of God. What is of man uses manipulation, outside pressure and instruction to make a person do what he should be doing. But what is of God uses the implantation of a new nature within the heart of a person, causing him instinctively to live like a Christian. Causing him to naturally follow after righteousness and true holiness.

Springing up within the heart of this new nature is an aspiration to know God and experience His presence in everyday living. The anonymous writer of the book *The Cloud of Unknow-*

*ing* emphasizes this truth. He says, "Man's highest perfection is union with God in consummate love, a destiny so high, and so pure in itself, and so far from human thought that it cannot be known or imagined as it really is."

The way into God's presence has been paved for us, beginning with the Old Testament. The Old Testament never promises anything that the New Testament does not deliver on. And so the purpose of the Old Testament is to guide us into the truth of who Jesus Christ really is.

Looking back over the past, beginning all the way back to the Garden of Eden, we will discover that God spared no pains in laying out for us this pathway. The purpose of God from the very beginning of creation is fulfilled in the regenerated heart of every believer who now can enjoy the manifest, conscious presence of the living God. The way into God's presence is the delight of the redeemed. It is where he belongs, naturally.

## A Glory Gilds the Sacred Page
### by William Cowper (1731–1800)

A glory gilds the sacred page,
Majestic like the sun;
It gives a light to every age,
It gives but borrows none.

The hand that gave it still supplies
The gracious light and heat:
His truths upon the nations rise;
They rise, but never set.

Let everlasting thanks be thine
For such a bright display,
As makes a world of darkness shine
With beams of heavenly day.

My soul rejoices to pursue
The steps of him I love,
Till glory break upon my view
In brighter worlds above.

# 9

# ENJOYING THE MANIFEST, CONSCIOUS PRESENCE OF GOD

*But Christ being come an high priest of good things to come, by a greater and more perfect tabernacle, not made with hands, that is to say, not of this building; neither by the blood of goats and calves, but by his own blood he entered in once into the holy place, having obtained eternal redemption for us. For if the blood of bulls and of goats, and the ashes of an heifer sprinkling the unclean, sanctifieth to the purifying of the flesh: How much more shall the blood of Christ, who through the eternal Spirit offered himself without spot to God, purge your conscience from dead works to serve the living God?*

HEBREWS 9:11-14

The full purpose of our salvation is that we might enjoy the manifest, conscious presence of God as well as He enjoys our presence. When we are enjoying the conscious presence of God, we are fulfilling the tenets of our salvation. The purpose of our redemption is to bring us into a right relationship to God in order that He might bring us into a conscious relationship with Himself.

Man, unlike any other of God's creation, is uniquely created to experience God. Not to know God and His intimacy is
to deny our fundamental purpose. Back in the Garden of Eden,
before man's fall, God did not come down in the cool of the
evening to fellowship with the birds and the deer and the flowers. He came to have fellowship with Adam and Eve.

I must point out that in the Scriptures there are certain basic truths upon which other truths are built. If we do not understand these basic truths, other truths simply become a caricature
and lose their significance in our life. No truth stands by itself,
but always in relationship with other truths of God's Word. This
is where heresy begins to develop when men separate one truth
from another truth. Once we get a grasp of the basic, fundamental truth of God's Word, then we can begin to understand the
rest of what the Bible teaches. This that I am talking about now
is one of those basic truths, that God made us for Himself that
we might know Him, live with Him and enjoy Him forever.

In spite of this, the human race has been guilty of revolt.
Men have broken with God, and the Bible teaches that we are
all alienated from Him. That is, we—the human race—are
strangers to Him. We have ceased to love Him, ceased to trust
Him and ceased to enjoy His presence.

Man's revolt has in no way changed this basic truth of
God's Word. From Genesis to Revelation we have the unfolding
of redemption. Some have correctly pointed out that this "red
thread" winds its way all through Scripture from beginning to
end. In the book of Revelation, this is explained to us, "And all
that dwell upon the earth shall worship him, whose names are
not written in the book of life of the Lamb slain from the foun-

dation of the world" (Rev. 13:8). We need to ponder this great truth that before man was created, before he revolted against God, redemption was established. Redemption simply brings us back into intimate fellowship with God. This fellowship bears with it certain fruit.

Because I am a personality, and God is a personality, I believe that we can have personal interaction with God—the interaction between one personality and another in love and faith and conversation, to speak and to be answered. It is no proof that we have great faith if we solemnly, glumly, grimly and coldly live our lives, saying, "I believe," and never have God give any response to our faith. There ought to be a response.

I know there are times when we walk by faith and not by sight. We never walk by sight, but we walk by faith sometimes when God, for His own goodness, has hidden His face from us for a moment. But He said, "In a little wrath I hid my face from thee for a moment; but with everlasting kindness will I have mercy on thee" (Isa. 54:8).

We must have again that presence. We must learn to live again in that presence—the manifest, conscious presence of God.

## Conscious Relationship with God

The difference between revival and every other state that is spiritual is that the church may know the manifest presence of God. It may be difficult to grasp that God is with the worst church in the city. By that, I mean, God is present there. "Whither shall I go from thy spirit? or whither shall I flee from thy presence? . . . if I make my bed in hell . . . thou art there" (Ps. 139:7-8). The difference has to do with God's manifestation. The worse the church is, the less evident will be God's manifestation. And the better the church, the more evident His manifestation. Our goal is to experience His glorious manifestation as we assemble to worship God.

Every church is going to have some sort of ambience when you walk in. In some churches, you will have the stained-glass windows, the beauty of the music and even the sonorous tones of the minister. All of this adds up to a certain sense of presence. You may feel this presence, but you are not necessarily conscious of the presence of God. In fact, much of this ambience keeps a person from experiencing God's true presence.

How many people on Sunday morning go to church, expose themselves to the ambience and come out of that church feeling pretty good about themselves and yet have never encountered the manifest presence of God? Liberal churches are always talking about how nice it is to turn and say, "Hello!" to our heavenly Father and then sing about the fact that this is our Father's world and all the stars sing about Him and the little buttercups talk about Him. It all sounds wonderful and uplifting. But the simple fact is, man and God are enemies until there has been reconciliation by a sacrifice that satisfies God.

As I have been pointing out, the most natural thing for a man is a relationship with God—a relationship that is vital and intimate in every aspect. The thing that is destroying this is man's revolt against God. How does God rectify this? To begin with, He did a work we call "redemption." The primary purpose of this work is to effect a reconciliation with Him; to bring us back to the place that we belong—the place that we have been created for.

Take Cain and Abel as an illustration of this. It was not that Cain was a bad man and Abel was a good man. In fact, they were both bad men. Abel knew he was bad, but Cain denied that truth and acted like he was a good man. He would have fit very well into most of the liberal churches today. He had a flippant attitude toward his relationship with God. Whereas, Abel came in humility and brought a sacrifice, looked up and said, "O God, I'm not worthy."

Abel pleased God, not because he was a good man, for he was not. But Abel took a bad man's place in the presence of a holy God. On the other hand, Cain did not please God, not because he was worse than Abel—they were both sinners born of the same parents—but because he assumed that he was all right when he was all wrong. He assumed there was nothing that came between him and God; but Abel knew there was. That is the difference.

The whole purpose in God's bringing us into a right relationship with Him is so that we might come into a conscious relationship with Him, so that we might be conscious of God and He of us.

## God's Plan to Meet with Us

I think that if the apostle Paul were alive today, he would get chased out of every town he preached in. Paul's message was simply to tell people that they are sinners, they are without hope and without God in the world, and the spirit of disobedience works in them. This is not the message people want to hear today. And yet, until people come to this point of view, they will never enter into God's plan to meet with them.

Until people are converted to Jesus Christ, they remain outside of God's plan for fellowship. They are without hope, sinners outside the wall; they acquire, spend, marry and give in marriage; build, plant, sow, harvest, tear down and build up; beget others like themselves and then finally die. They can live their whole lives without being too concerned about God, except when making political speeches or when it is convenient to use God for their purposes.

God has a plan in place to override this to bring us into fellowship with Him. To understand this, we must go back to the Old Testament again. In the Old Testament, we have a beautiful picture of God's plan to meet with us. The problem pointed out over and over again is that because of who God is, and who we are, there can be no meeting. But God takes the initiative to prepare the way so that He can meet with us and we can meet with Him and enjoy Him forever.

The picture of this is the Old Testament tabernacle. It is a beautiful illustration of how God wants to penetrate our world in order that we can penetrate His world. The tabernacle was an oblong affair with wooden walls made of acacia with a roof over it, and part of it made of the skins of animals. In this Old Testament tabernacle, we can see how meticulously God's plans were developed in order to accomplish His goal: fellowship with us.

Let me break down some of the aspects of the Old Testament tabernacle that illustrate this marvelous truth.

## The Lower Court

As we look at the Old Testament tabernacle, the first thing that catches our attention is the lower court. Geographically, this was outside the tabernacle proper. It was often called the court of the Gentiles. This refers to people interested in religion, but they keep their distance from God. They want to be associated with religion for its benefits, but they certainly do not want to be inconvenienced by religion.

In the court of the Gentiles the people came so far but they would not do what it takes to allow them to get inside where the presence of God was manifested. Many are like that today. About the only time they get to church is when a baby is born or when somebody gets married or when somebody dies. Some-one rather cynically pointed out that people go to church three times in their life. The first time, they throw water on them, the second time they throw rice on them and the third time they throw dirt on them. This seems to apply to the majority of peo-ple these days.

And so the outer court represents people who merely want to be casually associated with religion but they do not want to go all the way.

## The Inner Court

Then there is the inner court. The inner court consisted of two stations—an altar and a laver. The altar was a great brazen altar, not a pretty thing at all. It was a kind of topless furnace with a grate underneath. Beasts would be placed on that altar, with a fire underneath, and the beast would go up in an ugly smoke. That was the altar. There the lambs were offered, the beasts, the red heifer and the creatures that were brought to sacrifice. I do not think that part of the tabernacle was a pleasant place to be, and I do not think a priest's job was a pleasant job.

Some people want to depict religion as a very beautiful, lovey-dovey, flowery affair. They get very creative in their artistic expressions of religion. There are the stained-glass windows, beautiful paintings and poetry by the truckload—all in an effort to paint religion as something beautiful and artistic.

These same people accuse Christianity of being a "slaughterhouse religion." The altar in the tabernacle was not a picturesque sight but rather an awful sight with blood and flies all around it, and the stench almost overwhelming. It must have been a very unpleasant and terrible thing. These artsy people repudiate all of this gory mess found at the altar. To them, religion has to be pretty, beautiful, uplifting and positive without any sacrifice at all. And this is where the rub comes. They believe in a religion without sacrifice. The religion without sacrifice leaves men in their sins, separating them from any fellowship with God. Many are now embracing a cross-less Christianity, which is, in fact, not Christianity at all.

As unpleasant and terrible as the altar might have been, there is one place that I feel is more terrible than that. That place is hell. The Scriptures teach us that if a man is not redeemed by the blood of the Lord Jesus Christ, which was the only acceptable sacrifice to God, he certainly will spend his eternity in hell. When people sugarcoat Christianity, arrange it all very nicely and neatly and take away the slaughterhouse element from it, they have, in effect, taken away the cross.

The crucifixion of a man on a cross outside of the hills of Jerusalem must have been a repulsive thing. There just is no way to glamorize the crucifixion of Jesus Christ. Just like the altar in the Old Testament tabernacle was a gory and unpleasant mess, so the cross of Jesus Christ was unpleasant in just about every aspect of it. But the altar in the Old Testament tabernacle foreshadowed the cross of Jesus Christ, and pointed to the one and only acceptable sacrifice for God. To take away the reproach of the cross is to undo God's remedy for man's revolt. Not only was the altar in the inner court, but also the laver.

If you came into the inner court, the first thing you met was the altar. There the sacrifice was offered and the lamb died. Once you got past the altar with its stench and blood, you came to the laver. The laver was filled with water, and everything could be washed there. I might respectfully suggest that that laver looks like a huge punch bowl filled with water. And there they washed, as though God were saying, "You first have to come by the cross and by the blood, by the altar and by the laver, by the lamb that died and by the washing of water by the Word."

I submit that the inner court at first glance is not a very pretty sight. But then, this sin and rebellion in man's heart necessitating the sacrifice of the Son of God is not a very pretty sight either. As awful as man's revolt and sin is, so wonderful is the all-sufficient remedy, the sacrifice of the Lamb of God that takes away the sin of the world.

## Inside the Holy Place

Once a person went through the inner court, he came to another room. This was as far as anybody could come. A veil shut this off, and nobody could enter except the priest. Worshipers could come in where the altar and the laver were, and after they had come by the cross and by the cleansing, they would come into the holy place. Except a man be born again, he cannot see the kingdom of God. Except he repent, he cannot see the kingdom of God—that holy place. This was the privilege they now enjoyed. And there were three pieces of furniture in that holy place. One was the little light—the candlesticks. There were seven of them burning there. The other was the shewbread, the little table with bread on it. And the other was an altar of incense.

## The Light of the World

It is not difficult to know what all this means. I think the Church universal agrees that that light was the light of the Holy Ghost that lights every man that comes into the world. "I am the light of the world; and when you have come by the cross and been cleansed, then you're enlightened," says the Holy Ghost. In giving us this little object lesson, He says you can be enlightened. The light of the world is Jesus, and the light of the Holy Ghost shining there, the Sevenfold Spirit shining, made it light.

## The Bread of Life

There was bread there, called "shewbread." O the bread of the presence! Wonderful, I think. Jesus was there unseen, but feeding His people the bread of the presence. The sixth chapter of John tells all about that. They said, "Our fathers ate bread." Jesus said, "Yes, but the bread your fathers ate was only temporary bread. I have come that you might have bread and if you eat of it, you shall never die." And they said, "Give us that bread!" And He said, "I am the bread of life." Many turned and went away. They could not take that. It was too doctrinal, too strong.

If that had been a preacher preaching like that, they would have said, "We love our brother, but let's get rid of him. We think it is too strong to say that Jesus is bread." That is what it says, nevertheless, in figure and type in the Old Testament. It says it in blunt language in the New Testament. And the Church has agreed to it, at least nominally, down the centuries, for we have our Communion service and we eat of the shewbread while the light of the Holy Ghost shines around about us.

### The Altar of Incense

Then there is the altar of incense. What was that? Sweet-smelling incense was laid on that altar and burned, filling that little room with the sweet fragrance—a symbol of prayer. Isn't that a beautiful picture?

For me, this is what the local church ought to be—a place lighted by the light of the Word shed forth by the sevenfold Holy Spirit. And where we gather to eat of the bread of life—not only on Communion Sunday, which points it up, but all the time, every Sunday.

It's the place where the altar of incense sends up its sweet spirals of fragrant perfume, sweet to God and pleasant in His nostril, and the sound of prayer pleasant in His ear. It is the sight of an enlightened people gathered together that is pleasant to His eyes. This is the only kind of church I am interested in.

## Muted Light, Stale Bread, Odorless Incense

Right here I want to say something that will no doubt land me on the wrong side of popular Christian opinion. But I will say it anyway. I do not believe the church is the place for entertainment. With that said, let me explain what I mean.

We have churches today, in desperate need of attendance, advertising in newspapers for the world to come and enjoy "clean entertainment." We have, so the boast goes, what the world has, only ours is much cleaner and, to add insult to injury, in my opinion, it is family friendly. I am not totally against entertainment; I am just totally against entertainment in the church and entertainment used by the church to try to win the world. How can we battle the world if we have locked arms with the world?

From my reading of the Holy Scriptures, church history and Christian biography, I find that there is nothing in the church that appeals to the world, and nothing in the world that appeals to the true Church of Jesus Christ. Every revival in church history has occurred when the Church stood in stark contrast to the world around them. Our worship services should be so holy and so filled with a sense of God's presence that unholy men will be very uncomfortable. Now we have done it the other way around. The most unholy person in town can come into the church and feel quite comfortable. People should come to a church worship service not anticipating entertainment but expecting the high and holy manifestation of God's presence. When this begins to take place, several things will happen.

First, all the carnal and pseudo-Christians will let out a yell and head for the nearest exit. Attendance will plummet and the offerings will all but disappear. Many churches are not willing to pay this price. But then the next thing that happens is the church begins to draw in people with an insatiable hunger and desire for God. Tired of the trite entertainment style of the world they long, as the deer pants after the water brooks, for a real experience with God.

I believe, and I could be wrong here but I do not think I am, that God's people are hungry for the real spiritual food. They have had it with artificial light and hard, stale bread and odorless incense. They have had it with the cheap imitations imported from the world; they long for the reality of God's presence among them.

A little further explanation might be that here is the Church and the Kingdom. The traveler finds light and the child finds food and the priest is able to pray. You are a traveler on your way home, but you have light. Without some kind of light, even a little bit of light, the night can be horribly, frightfully dark. And Jesus said, "The night cometh, when no man can work" (John 9:4). The New Testament talks about the moral and spiritual state of the world as that of being a dark night. We travelers desperately need light.

That is the Church, and for that Church, I will give everything that I have. If I knew that that kind of Church could be in the world now, again—that is, the churches could become that kind of Church—I would not hesitate to give the blood out of my veins. I do not boast about it, but I think I could say that I would gladly do it. I know I have many other thousands of friends who would too. That we could have the Church again—purified and cleansed, so that when we walk in, we know we are walking in where the light shines, where there is bread to eat and where there is prayer to be made that goes to the ear of God with acceptance. That is the Church.

I love the Church, for this is what the Church is: a company of people committed to this faith, to this kind of belief, enjoying the manifest, conscious presence of God.

# I Love Thy Kingdom, Lord
## Timothy Dwight (1752–1817)

I love thy kingdom, Lord,
The house of thine abode,
The church our blest Redeemer saved
With his own precious blood.

I love thy church, O God;
Her walls before thee stand,
Dear as the apple of thine eye,
And graven on thy hand.

For her my tears shall fall;
For her my prayers ascend;
To her my cares and toils be given,
Till toils and cares shall end.

Beyond my highest joy
I prize her heavenly ways,
Her sweet communion, solemn vows,
Her hymns of love and praise.

Sure as thy truth shall last,
To Zion shall be given
The brightest glories earth can yield
And brighter bliss of heaven.

# 10

# THE "SANCTUM SANCTORUM" OF GOD'S PRESENCE

*Having therefore, brethren, boldness to enter into the holiest by*
*the blood of Jesus, by a new and living way, which he hath consecrated*
*for us, through the veil, that is to say, his flesh; and having an high*
*priest over the house of God; let us draw near with a true heart in full*
*assurance of faith, having our hearts sprinkled from an evil*
*conscience, and our bodies washed with pure water.*

HEBREWS 10:19-22

When a Christian breaks through the religious routine and experiences God's presence for the very first time, he no longer wishes to go back. He has found something so utterly satisfying that he loses his former attraction to the world and the things around him.

The sacred Scriptures give us a great illustration of this marvelous truth in the Old Testament tabernacle. The book of Hebrews goes to great lengths to show the New Testament parallel to the Old Testament tabernacle.

The Old Testament tabernacle was divided into several rooms. In the first room, the "sanctuary," were candlesticks and shewbread. A veil divided the next room, and behind was called the "holiest of all." Sometimes it was called the "holy of holies" and sometimes the "sanctum." The "sanctum sanctorum"—the holiest of all.

The Old Testament priest could come to the outer court and to the holy place. However, inside the holiest of all, the holy of holies, they could not come. Only one man could enter that holy of holies, and only once a year. Then he came with blood, which he sprinkled upon the mercy seat where the fire burned. Scripture teaches us that the death of Jesus was the rending of His flesh, which was the tearing of that veil that separated the people from the holy of holies. Now all of God's people can come in to God's presence.

What I most particularly want to emphasize in this holy of holies is the seat. There was a sort of cedar chest affair, and it was plated outside and inside with pure gold. Then there was a lid on that chest also made of pure gold with a collar around that lid with the four corners sticking up a little to give it artistic beauty. On that lid were two figures of the cherubim, holy creatures, made of pure gold. They stretched their wings, and their wingtips touched. Between the wingtips burned and glowed the awesome holy fire, which the sages have called the "Shekinah," meaning the "presence" or the "face." And that was God. That is why the careless crowd could not see it. They could not come in.

That is also why the average rank and file of the priesthood could not come in. Only the high priest could go in there, and with averted face look on that awesome presence once a year while he held in his hand a basin of blood, saying, "O Presence,

I ought to die. O Shekinah. O God, I ought to die, but I bring this blood as evidence that although I ought to die another has died for me."

This is the holy presence I want to focus on and why so many Christians are shut away from it. I read recently and carefully checked again to know that the words of the Old Testament translated "presence" and "face" are the same word. *The face of God.* "In thy presence is fullness of joy," as David says in Psalm 16:11. And you find all through the psalms the worshiping man of God celebrating his entrance into the presence and looking forward to the presence of God. And he talks about the face of God. And that passage for instance: "When thou saidst, Seek ye my face; my heart said unto thee, Thy face, LORD, will I seek" (Ps. 27:8).

That same word is "presence." "In thy presence is fullness of joy. Thy presence, Lord, will I seek. When my heart said unto thee, seek my face, my heart responded, thy face, thy presence, Lord, will I seek." It is the same.

What I am trying to present here is that there is an unseen presence, which is God, that holy one, that one in the midst of us, which theology sets forth in the doctrine of the divine eminence. It says that that holy presence once localized between the wings of the cherubim is now wherever His creation is.

There is a difference between a presence and a manifest presence. It is a fine difference between a man's presence and his face. The same word and the same relative meaning, but not quite. If a man comes into the room and keeps his back turned to you, you can say, "He was in my presence for half an hour," or "I was in his presence for half an hour." But you do not have much fellowship with a man who keeps his back turned to you.

It is when he turns his face to you that fellowship begins. There is a difference between God being present and God's face being manifest to His people.

Israel knew that God was in the midst of them, but the High Priest was able to go in with blood and look upon God's face only once a year, and then come back out and pull back a heavy veil. It took some men to push it aside. That veil was there to shut out the unqualified from that holy face. Then, when Jesus our Lord died, when He gave up the ghost, the veil of the temple was torn from top to the bottom. God Himself rent it with His finger from the top to the bottom, not from the bottom to the top, where it might have been done by a priest or an enemy; and it was forever removed. Poor Israel sewed that veil up and used it again, trying to undo what God had done by the death of His Son.

And so they have wandered all these centuries, shut out from the Presence by sewing a veil up again. God was telling the entire world, "My Son, My eternal Son, by the rending of His flesh and the tearing of the veil has opened the way for you to enter. Now there is nothing to keep you out of the Holy of Holies, where only a priest could go before; now, all of God's people can go."

The Bible teaches that all of God's presence is everywhere. The Bible teaches that God's face—God's realized, manifest, enjoyed presence—may be the precious treasure of all the people of God.

## What and Who Is This?

I must talk about God—God the Father, God the Eternal Son, and God the blessed Holy Ghost. And as God reveals Himself,

He reveals Himself in nature. This is the strong, the mighty One. He reveals Himself in the Scripture by various names: Elohim, Jehovah, Jehovah-nissi, Jehovah-jireh, Jehovah-rapha—and these various names set forth the various facets of His majesty and His glory. He is the one that captures our adoration and praise. David said, "One thing have I desired of the LORD, that will I seek after; that I may dwell in the house of the LORD all the days of my life, to behold the beauty of the LORD, and to inquire in his temple" (Ps. 27:4).

In the book of Hebrews, it is beauty; it is grace. One translation says, "The grace of the Lord." Anything that is graceful is beautiful. And the person of God is beautiful. And this beautiful, awesome presence was dwelling there, and the priest could push in past that veil once a year when nobody else could.

Is it ever possible to overdo the talking about the glory of Christ? About that presence as revealed in Christ? This Lord Jesus Christ, this wonderful, loving, self-sacrificing Lord Jesus, who is a star and a sun and a light, and as revealed by the Holy Spirit in human experience, is unutterably holy and unspeakably adorable.

I am afraid our lukewarmness about the person of Christ is a great proof that we do not know very much about Him in personal experience. I tell you, we cannot keep still about that which we love. That which we love supremely and above all else, we are going to talk about it a lot. I will never get over it; it is still a delight to me; it is still a pleasure I cannot get over. I do not try to get over it. I just enjoy it.

This ability to love is one of the few desirable things left in the world and it is tragic how it has been dragged down. The world has made romantic love to be a strange thing. But the Church has made its love of Jesus Christ to be its supreme fountain of joy. "For me to live is Christ," said Paul in Philippians 1:21. It is the nature of love to be enthusiastic to the point of even being a bit of a nuisance about the thing it loves or the one it loves. If you never mention the Lord in conversation with each other, is it not proof that you are not much concerned about Him? If in our conversation we do not have impulsive, warm statements to make about our relation to the Lord, can we not properly conclude, with charity, that it is because we do not know very much about Him?

You could not talk to David long until the Lord was in his mouth. You could not read anything David wrote for one minute or one-half minute or one-quarter minute until you ran into the Lord his God. It was the same with the apostle Paul.

When the Pharisees saw the man that Jesus healed standing among them, they could say nothing. It is hard to refute flesh-and-blood evidence. Certainly, there is always someone to give an answer to any theology that might be presented. Somebody can rationally explain what has just happened. Somebody has a believable answer. But there is never an answer to your growing faith. There is never any argument that is valid against the glowing, throbbing heart of a man.

I can prove to the young father that his little baby is only one more baby among millions, but I cannot stand up against the glowing face of the happy, young father. If a mother looks down upon that baby, it is not going to help her or me or the world to say, "You're looking down in joy on the face of your baby, but don't you know that 25 years ago, your mother looked down on you like that?" Or even back to Eve, when she looked down on Cain and Abel, smiled, and held them in her arms? That does not mean anything to somebody who does not rapturously love someone. A lot of theology can be brought up to prove that there is something wrong with a man like me who insists on coming into the presence of God and enjoying Him. I know it. But, before the glowing face of men and women who have been in the presence, there is a great deal of understanding. As one unknown author has stated:

Show me Thy face—one transient gleam
Of loveliness Divine,
And I shall never think or dream
Of other love than Thine.

Why do some stay outside so much? Why do some people not enjoy the presence of God? I think it is because of the veil in the way.

"But," someone might say, "the veil was taken away."

## What Still Hides His Presence

Yes, but we have to deal with two veils. God took one of them away when Christ died on the cross. There was one veil God put up to keep us out, but He took that away and said, "Come, enter boldly now." He has taken His veil away. But there is another veil—a veil that He did not make. It is the closely woven veil of carnal self. The sun shines in its brilliance all day, yet a cloud can shut out a city from its rays; just so the veil of self can shut out the face of God. It hides the face of God from the worshiping heart.

143

I do not hesitate to say that Christians spend their lifetime outside the veil. Though the veil has been rent away and is not there anymore (God has taken away that veil), we have sewed the veil up with our own busy little hands. We have put up a veil worthy of self-love, self-pity, self-trust, self-admiration, self-content and these other self-sins. Within every ransomed breast burns that flame that came from the fire that was before the wings of the cherubim. Our God is a consuming fire. And that little flame burning in the breast of every redeemed man longs to be reunited with that eternal flame: the fire of His presence. But that little flame of ours is hidden behind the veil of self.

The rank and file does not want to enter beyond the veil of self. It demands a life of holiness in order to enter.

If I might express it like this: I do not think the members of the Commonwealth all around the world would very much enjoy spending all their time in the presence of the Queen. Would you? I think everybody would want to bow and go through all the protocol and would be very happy and would tell about it for the rest of their lives. But I do not think very many would want to live every day in the palace. Then they would have to be on alert all the time. They would have to be dressed properly, watch their English, know all the etiquette and procedures of court. And it would just be a little too much for the average easygoing citizen to want to do.

You do not always want to stay dressed up; you want to relax and fall apart and put on an old pair of slippers with a tear in the side and be comfortable. In a similar vein, I think you are not spiritual enough to want to live in His presence, because you always have to be at your best. To be at your best, you have to have the robe of righteousness. You cannot wear the old dungarees or the old, sloppy shirt. To enter that awesome presence and live means that morally and spiritually, you have to be right. You have to be clean. That is why the average Christian is perfectly willing to wait for heaven to have the experience of always being in the presence of God.

I think that if the average Christian would tell the truth from the depths of his heart, he would have to admit that being in the presence of God all the time would be a bore. He would not be able to take it. He wants to relax and go to the world and the flesh, like Adam, and go back to the fleshpots of Egypt. It's just a little too much to demand of us, that we gird ourselves, go into the land and stay there. Yet that is what the Holy Ghost is pleading that we do.

> Let us therefore come boldly unto the throne of grace (Heb. 4:16).

> Having therefore, brethren, boldness to enter into the holiest by the blood of Jesus, by a new and living way, which he hath consecrated for us, through the veil, that is to say, his flesh; and having an high priest over the house of God; let us draw near with a true heart in full assurance of faith, having our hearts sprinkled from an evil conscience, and our bodies washed with pure water (Heb. 10:19-22).

The ordinary Christian is satisfied to live just a little removed from the presence of God. God has always had His

David, His Paul, His Stephen and those who would die to taste what one man calls the piercing sweetness of the love of God.

## Getting Beyond the Veil of Self

So, what can we do now? Briefly, first *hold faith in love.* This makes a man dear to God. Second, *come in full confidence.* Then, third, *turn your back on self.* These three things will go a long way in tearing down that second veil and exposing the soul to the presence of God.

François Fénélon (1651–1715) wrote, "Cut and tear and burn and destroy and spare nothing of the old flesh, of the old veil." Take away that veil from before your face. God is taking away the one He had up to shut you out. Now you take the one you had up to shut Him out. Tear, rend, cut and burn until there is nothing left of the old veil that shuts us out from His presence.

Unfortunately, many Christians settle for less than God's conscious, manifest presence in their daily walk. There is a strain of loneliness infecting many Christians, which only the presence of God can cure. Why do so many Christians shy away from the holy presence of God? God's face (His realized, manifested and enjoyed presence) may be the treasure of all God's people.

The struggle to come and stay in the manifest presence of God is well worth the effort. The one who breaks through the self-imposed veil will discover a waiting presence that will grace and bless his or her life with the pleasing aroma of adoration and praise for the rest of their earthly days.

# Within the Holy Place
## by Gerhard Tersteegen (1697–1769)

His priest am I, before Him day and night,
Within His Holy Place;
And death, and life, and all things dark and bright,
I spread before His Face.
Rejoicing with His joy, yet ever still,
For silence is my song;
My work to bend beneath His blessed will,
All day, and all night long—
For ever holding with Him converse sweet,
Yet speechless, for my gladness is complete.

# 11

# THE DIMENSIONS OF GOD'S PRESENCE

*For if the blood of bulls and of goats, and the ashes of an heifer sprinkling the unclean, sanctifieth to the purifying of the flesh: How much more shall the blood of Christ, who through the eternal Spirit offered himself without spot to God, purge your conscience from dead works to serve the living God?*

HEBREWS 9:13-14

Mark Twain famously said, "The difference between the right word and the almost right word is the difference between lightning and a lightning bug." It is very important that we get hold of the right words and know exactly what they mean. There has been a big effort in recent times to colloquialize Christianity. By that, I mean to get rid of all the old standard words we have used ever since English was spoken and put in their places words more familiar. When that happens, we lose the meaning when we lose the word that contains the meaning. Scientists and doctors know that.

Ornithologists use a specific Latin word to designate a certain bird. I don't know the Latin word we use to designate the bird we call "flicker." My father always knew it as a flicker or a wet hen, because when it began to say, "Wet, wet, wet, wet, wet," it was going to rain, which is why they called it a wet hen.

Then there is a bird called the "golden winged wood-pecker." Others call it a "high hole" because they go up high in the tree and dig a hole in the tree and put their nest in there. So, between the flicker, the wet hen, the high hole and the golden woodpecker, you would not know what to believe. The or-nithologist, however, designates a bird by one Latin term, which never changes. The result is, every time any scientist or student hears that term, he knows exactly which bird it is. I have given you only four names the flicker is known by. It could be known by a dozen or two dozen, and probably is over the North American continent, for it is found everywhere. But when you want to think accurately, you think in terms of its Latin name.

Theology is like that. If I talk about God as the "All Father" or as the "One Upstairs," or I use some strange or private name, it may mean anything to anybody. But if I say He is "God, the Father Almighty, maker of heaven and earth and all things vis-ible and invisible," and stick to that, then I know exactly what I mean. And regardless of how many weird occult religionists try to designate God by various names, if I give Him the name that He gives Himself, I always mean the same thing that He means. If I say "Jehovah," I mean Jehovah. And if I say "God, the Father Almighty," I mean God, the Father Almighty. It never changes.

Words are little pitchers, and each one is labeled. It is the business of the devil to pour out the true meaning of each lit-tle pitcher and pour in some other meaning. Imagine what would happen at your house for breakfast if a little pitcher with the word "cream" on it got emptied out and somebody put vinegar in it. If you reached over to the little old familiar cream pitcher that has been used for years, and poured vinegar in your coffee, it would ruin the coffee, of course. So, when we find a little theological word so familiar to the Church down the centuries, and it means a certain thing, then some bright young fellow pours that meaning out, rinses it and puts another meaning in, you do not know where you are. You are all confused, all mixed up. So, let us stay not only by the truth, but let us stay by the words that convey the truth.

Christian writers today are busy writing down to the people and making morons out of us. Have enough gumption and intellectual verve to learn the simple language of the Bible, that when the Word says "repent" it means a certain thing; and when it says "justified," it means a certain thing; and when it says "born again," it means a certain thing. Find out what it means. It would not take you a minute and half, and from that time on, until you die, you will know exactly what you mean when using that language.

## The Need for Salvation: A Self-Demonstrating Truth

Let us take this step by step and notice what it says in Hebrews 9:13-14: "Christ, who through the eternal Spirit offered himself without spot to God." This presupposes certain truths, and one of those truths is that the fall of man is a fact. This is one self-demonstrating doctrine. Not all truths are self-demonstrating.

Say you were visiting a friend you had not seen for 10 years. You heard they had a new child in the home, but you did not remember if it was a boy or a girl. If you looked up and saw a child about three years old and so dirty that you could not get him cleaned up, and yelling for something to eat, slugging his way through a clean kitchen, you would not say, "Is that a girl?" You would know better. That is a self-demonstrating male. He is demonstrating by his conduct that he is a boy. And the worst thing in the world for that fellow would be to call him a girl.

Some truths are self-demonstrating; that is, they demonstrate themselves. God says, "Man sinned and fell." Where is the evidence? The evidence of this truth is all around us. You can pick up a newspaper, listen to a news report and read the evidence of man's sinfulness. Present-day society is plagued with greed and avarice and arrogance. Sin is here. Scripture says so and the truth demonstrates itself.

The basic tenets of Christianity declare that man's moral revolt alienated him from God and banished him from the presence of God forever. The wedge between God and man is simply sin. That is what the Bible teaches.

You do not have to have the fall of man taught down to you. You do not have to have anybody write you a little story trying to incorporate that event to stir the unstirrable atoms within you. Anybody ought to know this and believe it and stand for it. Man is a fallen creature. We are not what we should be and not what we were. Sin is here, and hate and insanity and impermanence and criminality and war. They are all here in the world. That is one fact.

It presupposes another fact: that redemption of man is an accomplished act. And this was done by the Godhead. Only the Godhead could visit this fallen man, redeem him and restore him. It is without human collaboration.

Redemption was the work of the Trinity. The Fall was a work wrought by man alone, but redemption was a work wrought by God alone. Christ (that is, the Son), through the eternal Spirit (that is, the Holy Spirit), offered Himself unto God (that is, the Father).

Redemption is not a solo act; it involves the Father, the Son and the Holy Spirit. In teaching about the Trinity, we often separate them, but they are absolutely inseparable, particularly in this area of redemption. The Early Church Fathers recognized that and said, "We are not to divide the substance, though we are to recognize the three persons. The Father, the Son and the Holy Ghost are consubstantial. They are of one substance and cannot be separated."

It is impossible to think of the Father over here, doing a work; and the Son out there, doing another work; and the Spirit across there, doing yet another work. The Spirit and the Son and the Father always work together in whatever is done.

The Bible teaches that the Father created the heaven and the earth, and then turns around and teaches that the Son created the heaven and the earth, and then says that the Spirit created the heaven and the earth. And it is not contradictory, because the Father and the Son and the Holy Spirit work together in creation. And they work together in redemption, too. You will notice how the Trinity worked together when Christ was incarnated at the annunciation. The angel came and said that the "Holy Ghost shall come upon thee, and the power of the Highest shall overshadow thee: therefore also that holy thing which shall be born of thee shall be called the Son of God" (Luke 1:35). There were the three persons in the incarnation and at the baptism.

Many of the cults today call into question the doctrine of the Trinity. To do so a person must disregard certain parts of the Scripture. Take for example, the baptism of Jesus by John the Baptist. The Father spoke out of heaven, the Son stood on the bank of the river and the Spirit came as a dove from the Father to alight upon the Son. And the Father said, "Thou art my beloved Son" (Luke 3:22), and put the Spirit upon Him. So you have the three persons at the baptism of Jesus.

Look at the Scriptures that detail the death, burial and resurrection of Jesus Christ. Prominent in these activities are all persons of the Trinity. Jesus said, "Destroy this temple, and in three days I will raise it up." There was declaration that the Son would raise Himself up. Then He said, "This is the Father's will which hath sent me, that of all which he hath given me I should lose nothing, but should raise it up again at the last day" (John 6:39). And it is always taught that the Father raised the Son. Romans 1:4 teaches us that the Holy Spirit raised the Son. Again, we have at the resurrection all the persons of the Trinity, working in perfect harmony to do the work of God.

## Pulling Spiritual Weeds from the Soil of Truth

Likewise, in redemption, some errors exist, and I would like you to get the errors out of your mind. You say, "Why waste your time on errors? Why not preach the truth?" You might as well say to a farmer, "Why waste your time on weeds? Why don't you just plant corn?" If he plants corn and does not deal with the weeds, he will not have any corn after a while. One fellow wanted to know how to make the world a better world in which to live. "Well," a man said, "I could think of one way. I could make good health contagious." But good health is not contagious; rather sickness is contagious. You just wait around to catch good health. You will not catch it. You will get measles. So, it is not good health that is contagious. It is disease. And so it is in the world.

Take, for example, the simple country garden. A well-tended garden is a very lovely thing to behold. To see the nice even rows without a trace of a weed anywhere is a beautiful picture. That garden, however, would not produce a thing if it were not for the hard work of the gardener. Without the work of the gardener it will produce nothing but weeds and deprive tomatoes and corn their growth. God said to Adam, "Thorns also and thistles shall it bring forth to thee . . . in the sweat of thy face shalt thou eat bread" (Gen. 3:18-19). So, man's face has to sweat in order to keep the weeds out. Failure to deal with weeds jeopardizes the health of the garden.

If you are going to know truth, you are going to have to pull the weeds out so that truth can grow. Let's look at some of the weeds that have grown up in the spiritual garden. After clearing the weeds away, we will see where truth grows.

## Weed: Christ Is for Us, God Is Against Us

Some say that Christ the Son differs from the God the Father. That is one weed I want you to pull out of your mind, never allowing it to grow there. The misconception is that Christ is for us and God is against us. Never was there any truth in that at all. Christ, being God, is for us. And the Father, being God, is for us. And the Holy Ghost, being God, is for us. The Trinity is for us. It was because the Father was for us that the Son came to die for us. The reason that God is for us is why the Son is at the right hand of God now, pleading for us. The Holy Spirit is in our hearts. He is our advocate within. Christ is our advocate above. And all agree. There is no disagreement between the Father and the Son over man. Some say Christ is loving and kind, whereas God is stern and just. The Scripture does not endorse any such belief.

## Weed: The Old and New Testaments Contain Different Messages

It took me quite a little while to escape the feeling that the New Testament is the book of love and the Old Testament is the book of judgment. But I have gone through the Old and New Testaments and carefully counted the words, and I find three times as much about mercy in the Old Testament as there is in the New. There is equally as much about grace in the Old as there is in the New.

Back in the days of Noah, Noah found grace in the eyes of the Lord. As we read in the psalms, "The LORD is gracious, and full of compassion; slow to anger, and of great mercy" (Ps. 145:8). Grace is an Old Testament quality. And judgment is a New Testament quality. Read the twenty-third chapter of Matthew. Read the book of Revelation, Jude, and 2 Peter and see what they tell of the terrible judgments of God coming upon the world—New Testament judgments. God is a God of judgment and a God of grace. Both judgment and grace are in the New Testament. And both judgment and grace are in the Old Testament. God is always the same, without change: Father, Son and Holy Ghost.

## Weed: The Father and the Son Love Us in Different Degrees

Then there is the teaching that Christ won God over to our side by dying for us. Some people imagine that. I have heard evangelists tell about an angry God with His sword raised to destroy a sinning man, and Jesus rushes in and the sword falls on His head. He died and the sinner lived. It might be good drama, but its very poor theology, for there is not a word of truth in it. The Father "so loved the world, that he gave his only begotten Son" (John 3:16). And it was the love of the Father that sent the Son to die for mankind.

The Father and Son were in perfect, harmonious agreement that the Son should die for the sins of the world. I do not think I am far wrong if I should say that while Mary's son alone actually died on a cross, I believe that the heart of God ached and was as deeply pained as the heart of the holy Son. If you were a father and had a son, and that son were to be executed by hanging tomorrow morning, who would suffer the greater pain—the boy who died with a rope around his neck, or you? I believe your pain would be greater than his, for his pain would be brief and over, and yours would never be over.

So, when the holy Father turned His back, by the necessity of justice, on His Son, who was dying on a cross, I believe the pain in the heart of God was as great as the pain in the heart of the Son. And when they drove the spear into the side of Jesus, I believe it was felt in heaven at the right hand of God. Though only the Son died, yet the Father suffered because He was one with the Son.

## Weed: Only God the Son Was Active in Our Salvation

Then, of course, there is the idea that only one person had part in redemption. The truth is, all three persons of the Godhead had part in redemption. The Father received the offering at the hand of the Holy Ghost. And what offering was it? It was the Son, who was offered as a lamb without spot and without blemish. So all three persons of the Godhead had part in redemption, though the Son paid the redemptive price to the Father through the Spirit. Oh, the depths, the heights, the light, the darkness and the cataracts of love that flow down from the heart of God through His Son to mankind, by the Spirit!

# The Difference Between Salvation and Redemption

Redemption is an objective thing outside of you. Redemption is something that took place on a cross. But salvation is something that takes place inside of you. And so, when I have appropriated redemption, I have made it subjective. I have taken that which is external to me—redemption—and made it internal within me. That is salvation—redemption appropriated. And the three persons of the Godhead call the lost to salvation. The Son said, "Come unto me, all ye that labor and are heavy laden" (Matt. 11:28). And in John 6:44, it says, "No man can come unto me, except the Father which hath sent me draw him." In Revelation 22:17, it says, "The Spirit and the bride say, Come." The redemption wrought for us by the three persons of the Trinity becomes salvation when we heed the call of Father, Son and Holy Ghost and we come.

When Jesus sat down with sinners to eat bread, He knew why He was there. Others saw Him with sinners and said, "How is it that He eats with sinners?" He was there for the same reason the Salvation Army girl goes into a saloon. She is not going in there to get a drink. She is going in there to give the water of life. Jesus ate that way with sinners. He sat down with them everywhere, not that He enjoyed their wickedness, but that He wanted to help them.

# A Trilogy of the Trinity

## The Shepherd

Jesus told three powerful parables recorded in Luke 15, but they were really just one parable. Once there was a shepherd with a flock of sheep. Ninety-nine of them were safe in the fold, but He looked around and said, "There's one missing." He left the 99 safe and looked everywhere until He found the lost sheep.

## The Woman

Once there was a woman with a beautiful piece of jewelry composed of 10 pieces of silver. It broke and the jewelry scattered all over the floor. She searched everywhere to find them. When she had picked it all up, she said, "There's one piece missing." She got her candle and went searching everywhere, and finally she found it. "Ah!" she cried out, "I found it!" Everybody was glad she had found the missing piece.

## The Father

The third parable in the trilogy is about the father and the lost son. One of the sons was a young delinquent, and said, "Father, give me my share of my inheritance. I don't want to wait until you die. You may not die yet for years. Give me my share." The father gave him his share and he took it and went away and spent it. Later on, he got to lying around there, dirty, ragged and smelling of the pigpen, and said, "What a fool I've been. Boy, have I had it. Back home the very servants are properly dressed, clean and well fed. And here I am, lying in a hog pen. I know what I'll do. I'll go back home."

As he went, he composed his little speech. He said, "I'll tell my father, 'I am not worthy to be called thy son. I have sinned in they sight. Therefore, make me one of the hired servants.'" When he returned, the father saw him, ran to him, greeted him, gave him new garments, killed the fatted calf and had a feast in his honor.

## The Trinity's Collaboration

I've heard those three parables from the first time I can recall, but I never knew the meaning until years later when I had a session with God in earnest prayer: "O God, what does this mean?" I ignored the commentators, which is usually a good thing to do, and I sought God alone to find out what it meant. There came to my heart a revelation just as beautiful as when in flying, you break through the clouds and see the sun-bathed landscape below. I saw it all, and I see it now, and that was years ago, and I have had no reason to change my mind.

They were the three persons of the Trinity. That lost boy was the lost world. That lost coin was the lost world. That lost sheep was the lost world. And there was the Father looking for His lost boy. And there was the Son, the shepherd, looking for

His lost sheep. And there was the Holy Ghost, the woman with the light, looking for her lost coin. And they all added up to being the redeemed human race. Father, Son and Holy Ghost were all looking for the lost. The Father was waiting for His boy to come home. The Son was looking for His sheep. And this woman, this Spirit, was looking for the silver piece, the jewelry to wear around her neck. And so God said to me, "This is what it means. Father, Son and Holy Ghost are all busy searching for His lost treasures."

That is why Jesus talked to sinners. He was the Son looking for the sheep. His Father was looking for His boy. And the Holy Spirit was looking for the silver coin. Father, Son and Holy Spirit are united in this. Now, that to me is wonderful.

I hope you see that you have the answer to all the heretics and all the pitcher-emptiers and all the people who want to moronize you and write silly stuff. I know what I believe, sir. I believe that man fell, and God redeemed him, and in redeeming him, all three persons of the Trinity were engaged in the holy act of redemption. The Father received the sacrifice. The Son gave it. And the Holy Ghost conveyed it. So Father, Son and Holy Spirit, the divine Trinity, is engaged in saving mankind. I pray that we may be wise enough to know it and turn our eyes to Him. Follow this call today, for the night cometh when no man can work.

The manifested, conscious presence of God is a result of the collaborated effort of the Trinity. It is a harmony between the Trinity, and the man redeemed by the blood of the Lord Jesus Christ. God desires to reveal Himself to us more than we desire to experience His presence.

# Himself
## by A. B. Simpson (1843–1919)

Once it was the blessing,
Now it is the Lord;
Once it was the feeling,
Now it is His Word.
Once His gifts I wanted,
Now the Giver own;
Once I sought for healing,
Now Himself alone.

Once 'twas painful trying,
Now 'tis perfect trust;
Once a half salvation,
Now the uttermost.
Once 'twas ceaseless holding,
Now He holds me fast;
Once 'twas constant drifting,
Now my anchor's cast.

Once 'twas busy planning,
Now 'tis trustful prayer;
Once 'twas anxious caring,
Now He has the care.
Once 'twas what I wanted
Now what Jesus says;
Once 'twas constant asking,
Now 'tis ceaseless praise.

Once it was my working,
His it hence shall be;
Once I tried to use Him,
Now He uses me.
Once the power I wanted,
Now the Mighty One;
Once for self I labored,
Now for Him alone.

Once I hoped in Jesus,
Now I know He's mine;
Once my lamps were dying,
Now they brightly shine.
Once for death I waited,
Now His coming hail;
And my hopes are anchored
Safe within the vail.

# 12

# OUR MUTUAL FELLOWSHIP IN GOD'S PRESENCE

*Let us draw near with a true heart in full assurance of faith, having our*
*hearts sprinkled from an evil conscience, and our bodies washed with*
*pure water. Let us hold fast the profession of our faith without wavering;*
*(for he is faithful that promised;) and let us consider one another to*
*provoke unto love and to good works: Not forsaking the assembling of*
*ourselves together, as the manner of some is; but exhorting one another:*
*and so much the more, as ye see the day approaching.*

HEBREWS 10:22-25

Here we find four biblical assertions: "Let us draw near to God"
(Heb. 10:22); "Let us hold fast to our profession" (v. 23); "Let us
consider one another" (v. 24); and "Let us not forsake the assembling of ourselves together" (v. 25). These "let us" statements
mean, "Come on, we must do this." They are words of exhortation and urgency showing us our privilege and our duty.

Such words teach us that we cannot hope to deadhead into
spiritual advancement. We cannot ride on a pass. It requires
active exercise of our spiritual faculties. We simply dare not allow ourselves to hope that time will aid us. Time never helped

anybody yet, and never will. Time is the medium in which we may help ourselves or seek God's help, but time never helped anybody.

## We're Invited into God's Presence

"Let us draw near" means that we have something to do. If I might change the figure here, the whole work of God with men floats in the sea of grace and rests upon the foundation of grace, but it does not paralyze the human will and it does not exempt us from spiritual activities. "Let us draw near," He says, and it is to God that we are to draw near; and the great good news is that we can approach God. This is really the great good news of the gospel—that man can approach God again. Man, who went out of the Garden, at the stern command of God, can now come back with all his race into the presence of God again; and yet that approach is not one of physical distance.

It is very important that we know that our approach is not one of physical distance as if God were far off. When we make a pilgrimage to find Him, we act as though God were in some distant place on our world map, and we need to travel there, getting nearer to Him as we go, and going farther away from Him as we leave. Do not think of it like that. To do so is to think falsely. God is not far from any of us. "God is here, and the nearness to God that we talk about is not one of distance, it has to do with a rich person-to-person and soul-to-soul relationship. It has to do with trust, love and intimacy of heart."

If you allow one week of your life to pass by and you have not done something to draw near to God, you are not obeying the instruction here.

## We Live by Faith

The second assertion is "Let us hold fast our profession of faith" (Heb. 10:23). We would like to get a spiritual experience floating us on high, above all. We would like to go into orbit and be sure there was nothing to do but simply ride around. You do not go to heaven that way.

I once noticed an ad for a pair of shoes. According to the ad, you put them on and just walk around on air. People imagine the Christian life the same way. You are converted, blessed and then walk around on air for the rest of your life. You do nothing of the sort.

I know there is a wheel in the middle of a wheel up there somewhere, but Christians do not happen to be in that place yet. So, we do not go to heaven on wheels as the song says, "You Can't go to Heaven on Roller Skates." We cannot go to heaven any other way but by the simple, pedestrian way: walking by faith. The Lord does not talk about a flight of faith, nor does He talk about a tour of faith; He talks about a walk of faith.

The temptation to quit the journey comes to everybody. Some have been tempted to just give up the whole Christian life and be done with it. I suppose you feel very guilty about that, and you are; let me comfort you by telling you that you are not guilty all by yourself. People of God have that temptation come to them when things get tough, and they say, "What's the use of trying, anyhow? I can't do as I want to do, I can't serve God as I long to do." The temptation is to quit. But people are ashamed to admit it.

If their testimonies were as frank as they should be, many a man, instead of getting up and saying, "Pray for me that I may hold out faithful and so on," would say, "I was tempted last week to give up this whole deal, but the Lord helped me, and I didn't." That would be frank; it would be a little difficult to do that, because we are taught to win friends and influence people and never tell the truth at all. We are trained to say the thing we are supposed to say rather than the honest thing. The pressure is just so great that we almost look up to God as Elijah did and say, "God, I've had it. There isn't any use, Father, take me; there's nobody around that's any good."

We are tempted like that sometimes, but I have a little key for you. I usually do not hand out keys, but I have a little secret of how you hold fast the profession of your faith. It is so down-to-earth and common that it will disappoint you, but it is good. *Just outlive your troubles.* I have outlived so many things, so many people that did not like me; I just outlived them. You just go right on outliving your difficulties.

That neighbor who slams the door all hours of the night and morning and turns the TV on until it comes roaring through the partition until you say, "Oh, God, what will I do?" Just outlive him. He will move; you just keep right on where you are.

That neighbor whose dog howls incessantly, tied to a tree out there; just keep right on living. Go right on. He will move, God will take him somewhere else, and so with everything else that tempts you to want to quit.

How about that boss you work for that you just do not know how you can continue to go to work? You do not mind the work, but you just wish you were somewhere else, and you are shopping around for another job and cannot find one. You just keep right on walking with God, and one of these times something will happen. That fellow will be moved to some other town; he will get blessed; he will get to liking you or the problem will untangle. You just keep on; it will not kill you if you walk on with God.

"Let us hold fast," says the Word of God. But it also says, "to the profession of our faith." The profession of our faith has its ramifications right down in our living; so you just wait around, it will come out right.

A dear old brother with not too much education, but he was a dear saint, said the passage of Scripture he loved was, "It came to pass." He testified, "When I get in trouble, I just look up to God and say, 'Father, I remember this came to pass.'" It passes after a while, and all of your problems come to pass. They will pass if you'll just outlive them and keep right on.

## We Urge Others to Love and Good Works

Then the other assertion is, "Let us consider one another to provoke unto love and good works" (Heb. 10:24). We have serious responsibilities for other people. God has laid the welfare of others upon us, and He will hold us responsible. I suppose one of the most insolent and cynical statements or questions in the entire Bible was Cain's question after murdering his brother: "Am I my brother's keeper? Why are you asking me about my brother? Do I have to take responsibility of him on my life?" Yes you do, you take the responsibilities of others on your life. We should be responsible before all men for our lives, for our example, for our word. We should be responsible to rouse people, incite people and urge people on in their Christian walk.

Some Christians have a bad effect on other Christians. One Christian will get with another Christian and they have to fight to keep up their spiritual lives, this one Christian drags them. There are those rare Christians whose very presence is an incitement to you to want to be a better Christian. That is what it says here: "Let us consider one another to provoke." Provoke, of course, means to stir them up to love and good works.

## We Do Not Abandon Assembling Together

The fourth assertion is, "Not forsaking the assembling ourselves together" (Heb. 10:25). There is a significant mark of a lack or relish for the apostolic assembly. When going to church becomes a problem, something is wrong. When the circle of believers becomes too dull, many excuses are given, but there is only one; we have cooled off in our spirit. The thing that Christian's have always done is come together to worship and pray and to reminisce and to anticipate and to search the Scriptures and to sing holy hymns and testify. This has been done from the day of Pentecost to the present hour. When I become a Christian and I am not led by a magnetic attraction to the circle of believers, something is wrong with me.

I believe the church is the assembly, the church of God, and there are reasons for our assembling. We are not simply doing this out of habit or because it is a custom that we cannot get over. We do it because there are reasons for it.

By nature, Christians are gregarious. "Being let go they went to their own company" is a sentence characteristic of the people of God, as well as sinners. People always go to their own company, and so it is perfectly normal for us to want to do so. All the beasts of the jungle meet at the waterhole, and there is a strange truce there; although they fight to the death in the jungle, when they go to the waterhole, there is a truce; they all meet together where there is the water. And God's people meet at the waterhole; they meet together where the fountain flows. They are gregarious. Those who raise sheep know the sick sheep is the only one who does not like the flock. He wanders off by himself behind the bush and dies. The healthy sheep all like to be where the other sheep are.

The second reason is that we need each other. The individual Christian needs the company of Christians. God can say to a company of Christians what He cannot say to an individual Christian, just as He can say to the individual lonely praying soul what He cannot say to the company.

If your Christianity depends upon the pastor's preaching, then you are a long way from being where you should be. If you do not have a private, secret conduit, a pipe leading into the fountain where you can go anytime all by yourself, whether there is a pastor there or not, whether you have heard a sermon in a year, you have nevertheless an anchor; you have a root, you have a conduit, you can get the water from God. But over against that, and supplementing it and correcting it, is this truth that God can say to you in church what He cannot say to you all alone.

God can take a man onto a mountain and talk to him and then send him down where the people are and talk to him and say to him down there what He could not say up there. So we must close the door and have private prayer; but we need to have our private prayers corrected and brought into symmetry by the public prayers. We need to read the Scriptures all by ourselves, and then we need to hear the Scriptures expounded in the public assembly.

Christ went to the synagogue regularly. People write me something like this, "Mr. Tozer, the town where I live doesn't have a single gospel church. I'm a born-again Christian; what will I do?" I write back and remind them that Jesus went to the synagogue, as was His wont. He had the habit of going to church on the holy days and went even though He did not agree with much He found there. He went because He wanted to be in the company of people who, at least essentially, were worshiping God. So you go ahead, the Lord will arrange it somehow, you will hear truth. Christ went to the company regularly, and so should we. Christ promised special blessing to the company where two or three are gathered in His name (see Matt. 18:20), and the assembly of God's people is an historic tradition.

Why Christians go to the assembly only occasionally is beyond my comprehension. Suppose you were in Russia and did not like the way they were doing things. You did not like their communistic system, their secret police; you did not like anything about Russia at all. Then, while walking one day in the country you noticed a little, old building that looked forsaken. While walking by you heard a noise and said to yourself, "I believe that's English. I believe they're singing." When you went close to the door, you notice what they were singing. They were singing "God Bless America." As you peeped in you recognized American faces all around you.

There all by themselves, shut away, Americans from here and there gathered together for a little while in fellowship. Huddled together were a couple dozen Americans. And you burst in on them with a big smile and some of them recognize you. Soon they sing a hymn together and you begin to talk. "Oh, yes, I used to live in Chicago. Have you ever been down at such and such a place?" Soon you have a fellowship way across the ocean, way over in that big continent there where it snows. Oh, how good you would feel! Then you would shake hands and say, "I've got to go back to the grind, to the secret police." You would shake hands and part and say, "Next week let's meet again."

Don't you see how perfectly normal that would be? Don't you see you would live for it? You would say during the week, "I have to be out here with people whose language I do not know or like, and people who are suspicious of me. Out here I don't like this, but, oh, I live for the time when I can go back into that little building and sit and chat and reminisce and talk over old times and sing good songs with my friends." That is a natural thing, nothing wrong with that; that is delightful. And isn't it true that here we Christians are a minority group in a great big sinful, Godforsaken world, or almost Godforsaken, for they have driven Him out and refused to have His reign over us.

During the week, we go to school, we work, we sell, we buy, we tend store, we drive trucks, we do something all week long under the pressure of it. But if we know where there is a company of people who think as we think, whose hearts are like our hearts, who love what we love, who are our people, whose faces are recognizable—we know who they are and we like to shake their hands and smile at them, don't you think that is reason enough for everybody to go to church every time they can, allowing only sickness to keep them away?

I love the people of God. Sometimes I have to get after them a little bit, but I love them. I love the kingdom of the church. But when people do not practice it, when they go infrequently or intermittently and say, "I can serve God under the trees," that is a bromide, a cover-up, an excuse, and it only hides a cold heart.

Usually, when a Christian loses his love for the company of saints, he rationalizes; he blames the minister, the music, the unfriendliness of the people, the hypocrites in the churches, or the church building. The people draw him, the people whose spirit he has, he is with them. The wife pops in their little car and drives off to the church and she goes among her people. Why is she faithful? Because she recognizes her own people; she loves them. I love the church of Christ. I am commissioned to love it, to scold it, to warn it and to feed it and pray for it.

## Corporate Delight in God's Presence

So now there are four assertions: "Let us draw near to God"; "Let us hold fast to our Christian profession"; "Let us consider one another" and be responsible to help each other; and "Let us not forsake the assembling of ourselves together," for the sweetest place in all the world is the assembly of the saints.

Thank God, for freedom in a land like this where there are no secret police listening to what we say, ready to catch us and condemn us because we dared to talk about God to a people who wanted to hear about it. Thank God for freedom such as ours. Let us not sell it out or neglect it. Let us take advantage of our freedom to worship God among the people of God.

The worship of God's assembled people is a collaboration of individuals committed to God's presence, and He to theirs. What we have experienced individually, He has connected when we come together to delight in God's presence among the assembly of believers.

## Ten Thousand Times Ten Thousand
### by Henry Alford (1810–1871)

Ten thousand times ten thousand,
In sparkling raiment bright,
The armies of the ransomed saints
Throng up the steeps of light:
'Tis finished, all is finished,
Their fight with death and sin:
Fling open wide the golden gates,
And let the victors in.

What rush of hallelujahs
Fills all the earth and sky!
What ringing of a thousand harps
Bespeaks the triumph nigh!
Oh, day for which creation
And all its tribes were made!
Oh, joy for all its former woes
A thousand-fold repaid!

Oh, then what raptured greetings
On Canaan's happy shore!

What knitting severed friendships up,
Where partings are no more!
Then eyes with joy shall sparkle,
That brimmed with tears of late;
Orphans no longer fatherless,
Nor widows desolate.

# 13

# The Threat to Our Delighting in God's Presence

*For if we sin wilfully after that we have received the knowledge*
*of the truth, there remaineth no more sacrifice for sins,*
*but a certain fearful looking for of judgment and fiery indignation,*
*which shall devour the adversaries.*

HEBREWS 10:26-27

Hebrews 10:26 has widely been misunderstood and generally misinterpreted. It appears to be out of accord with the rest of the Scripture, although it is not. When you find a verse of Scripture that seems to contradict another verse of Scripture, always remember that it does not. The contradiction is in your mind because you do not have sufficient light. If you had sufficient light you would know there is no contradiction there.

This passage has been used as a club by irresponsible preachers to frighten some of the Lord's people. And some of the Lord's sensitive and badly frightened people have used it against themselves. Not only has this passage been misused by people against others, and against themselves, but Satan, the devil, uses this passage to malign God and create the impression that God is a short-tempered tyrant who rules according to His own unreasonable and unpredictable whims.

The devil also uses it to trap the consciences of people. There is hardly a passage anywhere in the Bible that more people inquire about than this one. These are usually very serious-minded, honest people whose consciences have been trapped. A free conscience may lead to repentance, but a trapped conscience can only lead to despair. Satan uses Scripture as a trap to ensnare the people of God. Some would say, "If it's Scripture, how can it be used as a trap?" Remember what Peter said:

> And account that the longsuffering of our Lord is salvation; even as our beloved brother Paul also according to the wisdom given unto him hath written unto you; as also in all his epistles, speaking in them of these things; in which are some things hard to be understood, which they that are unlearned and unstable wrest, as they do also the other scriptures, unto their own destruction (2 Pet. 3:15-16).

When he says "the unlearned," he does not mean people who have not gone to college, but people who are not deeply learned in the Scriptures. The result is that their consciences get in trouble and they turn against themselves and use this passage of Scripture to beat themselves down. I know who is doing this; it is the devil.

This situation prevents many a prodigal from coming home. If someone had gone to the prodigal son (his story is told in Luke 15) and told him there was a passage of Scripture that said if you left your father's house and went into the far country there remains no more sacrifice for sin, he would never have come back. He would have misunderstood it and, if not an honest man at least a sensitive man, as the passage shows, he would never have come back to the father's house.

Another thing this passage does, it tends to draw away tension from major truth to minor truth and to create argument and bitter feelings. It is astonishing how the whole Sermon on the Mount can be passed over and people argue over this one verse of Scripture. It has been misunderstood, misinterpreted and misused both by the devil and by people against the people of God.

## What this Passage Does *Not* Mean

I am always on the side of the people of God. I sound sometimes as if I am not, because I am severe with them. I am severe with them as a father is severe with a little family of children that he loves to death and of which he is very proud. I am very proud of God's people and very happy to be with them and recognize them as being the Father's children. But I am not going to let them get away with a lot of bad manners and bad habits when they should not. For that reason, I am severe, but I am severe with a smile. I never preach except with a smile in my heart and with the joy that I am part of the Church.

Hebrews 10:26-27 says, "For if we sin willfully after that we have received the knowledge of the truth, there remaineth no more sacrifice for sins, but a certain fearful looking for of judgment." First, let's look at what it does not mean. If we can determine what it does not mean, we are in a better position to find out what it does mean. Well, it does not mean that only sins done before hearing the gospel can be forgiven. It does not mean that if after you hear the gospel and are enlightened, and you sin willfully, there is no more chance for you ever to be saved. It does not mean that we had one chance to hear the gospel; and we heard the gospel and were not converted but went on in sin, so there is no more sacrifice for sins remaining. Now that is what it does not mean, because that interpretation would violate all the Scriptures and destroy the long-suffering and patience of God.

How many Christians were converted to Christ the first time they heard the gospel? How many were converted the second time, the third time, or the tenth time they heard the gospel? Some taught in Sunday School before conversion, and some were giving money to foreign missions and sending out the gospel that they did not understand themselves before they surrendered to God and gave their heart to the Lord Jesus Christ to be their Lord and Savior.

If this passage meant that you are done when you have once heard and understood, for that is what the word "enlightened" means, and after that you sin, everyone would be ruled out for salvation. I do not think anybody is converted the first time they hear the gospel. Some people wait a long time. I wished they did not.

And it does not mean that only sins done before hearing the gospel can be forgiven; if it meant that, then God would be requiring us to do what He would not Himself do. Because He told us that we are to forgive other people 70 times 7 times. And if we are to do that, and He demands it of us, then I would assume He would do it Himself; so this rules out any such def-inition or interpretation as the one I have suggested. And it does not mean that if a Christian sins, there is no hope after that, because that would be to contradict the Scriptures again.

Now what is the ideal? The ideal is that the Lord's people should not sin at all. Jesus Christ came that He might destroy the works of the devil. And so, "My little children, these things I write unto you, that ye sin not. And if any man sin, we have an advocate with the Father, Jesus Christ the righteous: and he is the propitiation for our sins: and not for ours only, but also for the sins of the whole world" (1 John 2:1-2). That is written to Christians, and you cannot dispensationalize that out.

If it were true that if a Christian sins willfully after he is converted—after he has heard the knowledge of the truth—it doesn't say converted, that he has heard the knowledge of the truth or been enlightened, then why do we have 1 John 2:1-2?

Peter certainly did not accidentally curse, swear and deny his Lord. There was no accident there. Peter was sneaky and wanted to get out of difficulties; so when the people with him in the courtyard said, "Are not you one of his disciples?" Peter saw that the Lord was in trouble and he did not exactly want to be in trouble too, so he just lied his way out of it. He sneaked out the easy way. It was a bad thing to do; he repented after-wards in bitter tears and the Lord forgave him. In fact, he was the first one the Lord hunted up after He rose from the dead. Peter, the one who needed Him the most.

If it were true, as some would say, that if after you have heard the knowledge of the truth and been enlightened, and you sin, there remains no more hope for you, then what about

Peter? And what about the universal experience of religious people? I do not advocate a person backsliding, and I never want to drop one lonely word that would encourage any child of God to leave home. I do not want to encourage anybody in any measure to do wrong. Rather, I want to encourage them to do right and always to walk in the Spirit and not fulfill the lust of the flesh. However, the simple fact is that some of the Lord's people do backslide.

## Compare All Scripture to Get at the Truth

Keep in mind that one passage of Scripture is never enough to establish a doctrine. It takes more than one Scripture to establish a doctrine. Here is the rule: If this verse says it and this verse confirms it, then you are likely to be right in your doctrine, but you don't have the truth. But if you go over here and you find it, and you go over there and you find it, and you go back there and you find it, and you go on forward and find it, and the verses all say the same thing, then you know you have the truth.

Take for example the love of God. John 3:16 is not enough to establish the doctrine of the love of God. But go back to the book of Deuteronomy and hear God say, "And because he loved thy fathers, therefore he chose their seed after them, and brought thee out in his sight with his mighty power out of Egypt" (Deut. 4:37).

Go on into the book of Psalms and the book of Isaiah and hear the Holy Spirit talk about the love of God. Go on into the Prophets and hear Isaiah talk about it. Then go into the New Testament and hear Christ and the apostles talk about it, and on through Revelation. When you see the same message in all those places, you know you have a doctrine you can trust; you know you have doctrine you can live on and die on world without end. But never reach into the Bible and get one verse to make that verse either hope or despair, because it is not enough. Every Bible school, every seminary knows that dogmatic theology is built upon the harmony of more than one verse of Scripture.

When the devil took Jesus up onto the pinnacle of the temple and said, "Jump off of here, because it is written, 'he shall give his angels charge concerning thee,'" our Lord's response was, "Again it is written, thou shalt not tempt the Lord thy God" (see Matt. 4:5-7). Truth lies not in "angels shall keep thee." It lies in, "the angels shall keep thee, but don't tempt God."

When God promises to hear your prayers, it does not mean He makes an unconditional promise to answer them the way you want them answered. Other passages of Scripture tell you He will answer your prayer if you will meet the terms and pray in His will. So we get the truth not by riding one passage, but by taking all the Scriptures and putting them together.

That is why the passage in Hebrews 10:26 does not mean what it does not mean. Now what does it mean?

Look at two words here: "sin" and "sacrifice." The sin held up here is the sin of unbelief. In the book of Hebrews, you will find that the sin being referred to here is the sin of unbelief in the Word of God. This is a sulky stubborn refusal to go on.

Israel in the Old Testament took a vote of no confidence against God. The writer to the Hebrews warns not to do as they did. "To whom was he grieved these forty years." Even those that sinned in the desert, whose carcasses fell in the wilderness and to whom He swore they should not enter into His rest but to them that believed not. So we see that they could not enter in because of unbelief. Basic unbelief was the trouble of the Jew, and so the writer to the Hebrews says, "You are Hebrews and have in you the streak your forefathers had when they voted no confidence in the olden days even though they had sacrifice there." They had the sacrifice made by the priests.

In Jesus Christ there had been a fulfillment of all those sacrifices. The Old Testament Jews used to offer their sacrifice and be forgiven for their sins, and if they sinned again, they offered another lamb and another lamb; but now, says the man of God, there is no more Old Testament sacrifice. Do not go and look to our old sacrifices, for they are out, they have no meaning because they have been fulfilled in Christ. "For the law having a shadow of good things to come, and not the very image of the things, can never with those sacrifices which they offered year by year continually make the comers thereunto perfect . . . but this man, after he had offered one sacrifice for the sins for ever, sat down on the right hand of God" (Heb. 10:1,12). Therefore, there is no other sacrifice. And if you insist on going back and are always full of unbelief and stubbornly rebel, if you turn away now from this last final sacrifice and go back to your altars, your altars do not count, for there is no more sacrifice for sin.

Either it is Jesus Christ, or there is no sacrifice. There is no place to go if you go on in your sin; do not imagine you can go back and start over and offer another lamb and go back to an altar. You cannot do it, says the Holy Ghost here through the writer of Hebrews. But if you are looking for a judgment for all of us, it is this: either Christ or eternal loss. If we draw back from Him and still sin and go on willfully and refuse to go on with Him, there is no place else, there remaineth no sacrifice for sin. The old sacrifices of the Hebrews were out, so it is Jesus Christ our Lord or else eternal loss or a fearful looking forward to a judgment that shall devour the adversaries.

There is no place to hide. As for the counterfeit hiding places people create for themselves, it is impossible to hide from the judgment of God. If you refuse the blood of Jesus Christ and look around for a hope somewhere else, as these people in the book of Hebrews were tempted to do, you are looking for another sacrifice, which has been done away with and ruled out.

The book of Hebrews is a book of complete repudiation of all the Old Testament sacrifices, establishing Jesus Christ the Lord as the one and only sacrifice. And no matter how many willful sinners there might be, the blood of Jesus Christ still cleanses us from all sin. What other kind of sin would there be except willful sinning?

When a man loses his temper, does he do it willfully? I suppose not. But if he loses his temper and beats his neighbor up, at just what point does it cease to be spontaneous and become willful? I do not think God makes an awful lot of difference between a sin that is a spontaneous burst of anger or lust and any other kind of sin. If a man wills to do and continues to sin and turns back to old Israel and to the altars, unto the old sacrifices, the man of God said, "Don't do it, they don't exist anymore; there remains no sacrifice. Go on to perfection, seek Jesus Christ who is your Lord and who offered a sacrifice for sin forever."

## No Place to Hide but in the
## Blood of the Lamb

When people say, "God is too loving to damn," I enjoy torpedoing that, for that is a phony hiding place. They say, "I don't believe there is a hell." I would like to torpedo that one as well, for that is also a phony hiding place. There is no place to hide. So hide in the blood of the Lamb. Outside of that there is no place to hide and no sacrifice to sin, no penitence, no righteousness, no doing good, no offering up of a lamb, no slaying of a pigeon or red heifer. It is all over now; there is no hiding place.

If you are nervous and sensitive, when you feel you have failed God or even whether you have or not, the temptation is to take it all to heart and begin to blame yourself. If you let that crystallize into a state of morbidity, you can hate yourself, condemn yourself, refuse to forgive yourself and refuse to believe that God forgives you to a point where you are a mental wreck.

Religion did not make you like that. You were like that and would not let religion straighten you out. But there is only one sin that cannot be forgiven, and that is the sin of attributing the works of the Holy Ghost to the devil—that is the unpardonable sin. That is the only one that cannot be pardoned. All sins shall be forgiven unto the sons of men except the one that is the unpardonable sin, and that is not what we are speaking of here.

Always remember this: The worried Christian has not committed the unpardonable sin. For it is part of the psychological state of the man who has committed the unpardonable sin that he does not know he has done it. And when you hear anyone grieving for fear they have committed the unpardonable sin, you can always be sure they have not. In the Bible, the ones that did were arrogantly sure that they were righteous and would laugh aloud if you told them they had committed the unpardonable sin. And the poor, grieved, sin-bruised people who wept at the feet of Jesus, thinking they might have committed the unpardonable sin, they had not.

So, if you should be among those who are so sensitive and so nervously distraught that you feel hurt and self-condemned and maybe wonder if you have committed the unpardonable sin, and you are pondering the meaning of "there is no more sacrifice for sin," the two do not mean the same. A troubled mind can always make them the same. But remember the rule of thumb: If you are worried, you have not committed the unpardonable sin. If you have committed the unpardonable sin, you are not worried that you have.

The degree of our delighting in God's presence rests upon our knowing our standing before God. It is no secret that the devil hates our joy in the Lord and will strive with all his power to rob us of this holy delight. Nothing bothers the devil more than a Christian delighting in God's presence.

I hope this truth will encourage God's poor troubled sheep; but I also hope it will not encourage them to be careless, for we do not want to be careless Christians. We want to walk circumspectly, for the time of that final day is drawing nigh. We want to be cheerfully hopeful because of the goodness of God and because of the infinite efficacy of the blood of the Lamb. We need no other sacrifice for sin.

# Only Believe
## by Paul Rader (1879–1938)

Fear not, little flock, from the cross to the throne,
From death into life He went for His own;
All power in earth, all power above,
Is given to Him for the flock of His love.

Fear not, little flock, He goeth ahead,
Your Shepherd selecteth the path you must tread;
The waters of Marah He'll sweeten for thee,
He drank all the bitter in Gethsemane.

Fear not, little flock, whatever your lot,
He enters all rooms, "the doors being shut,"
He never forsakes; He never is gone,
So count on His presence in darkness and dawn.

Only believe, only believe;
All things are possible, only believe,
Only believe, only believe;
All things are possible, only believe.

# 14

# Maintaining Our Spiritual Confidence in God's Presence

*Cast not away therefore your confidence, which hath great recompence of reward. For ye have need of patience, that, after ye have done the will of God, ye might receive the promise. For yet a little while, and he that shall come will come, and will not tarry. Now the just shall live by faith: but if any man draw back, my soul shall have no pleasure in him. But we are not of them who draw back unto perdition; but of them that believe to the saving of the soul.*

Hebrews 10:35-39

The key to maintaining our experience in God's presence is a spirit of fervency. Coming into the presence of God is only half the battle. Staying there is the most difficult part. Many things will cross our path to hinder our progress and avert our attention away from this, mostly a life full of occupation. Our fervency in this area needs the proper fuel or it will give out.

A Christian can be beat to death very easily by always focusing on the danger side of things and never admitting or acknowledging any good when it is found. The man of God who wrote the book of Hebrews did not make that mistake. Neither did our Lord. But while they were very faithful to rebuke, chasten, exhort and warn, at the same time they were very careful to encourage. We have here an encouraging passage of Scripture. This is for your encouragement. The writer to the Hebrews says, "Call to remembrance the former days" (Heb. 10:32).

Here is the correct use of "remembrance." It is to unite our yesterdays with our today and our tomorrows. If we had no remembrance of what had been, we would be vegetables and not men. By the mystery and wonder of remembrance, we make yesterday today and today will be tomorrow. Because our memory unites things, our human life is like a painting.

A painter begins with his canvas in one corner or at the top or bottom, and lays stroke after stroke and line after line and color upon color and shade upon shade. When it is all finished, he has a painting composed of all the brushstrokes he gave it during the time he was painting it.

Human life is very much like that. What if a painter laid on a brushstroke and then, when he dipped in the paint for the next brushstroke the first one disappeared? And that continued all the way through the painting. When he put on number two, number one disappeared; when he put on number three, number two disappeared. When he was finished, he would have a blank canvas. The only stroke would be the last one he laid on, and it would disappear shortly. Life is not like that. Life is to be a composite of all of its experiences so that we are to call to remembrance, and that is the correct use of "remembrance."

Some say we should not remember at all, and they quote

the apostle Paul who said that he forgot the things that were past (see Phil. 3:13). This is a misunderstanding, because we are forcing a statement out of its context. Any figure of speech or any passage of Scripture, if forced out of its proper meaning and not corrected by other passages of Scripture will lead you wrong. For instance, if you take the word "leaven" and make it to always mean something bad, then you take that authority on yourself to do that. But if you do, you will miss much of the meaning of the Scripture.

Take the expression "dead in sin." The Bible says, "But she that liveth in pleasure is dead while she liveth" (1 Tim. 5:6). Because the Bible teaches about sinners being dead, some therefore claim that a person is dead. He is unable to think, to help himself, to reason or to want to do right. He cannot make up his mind to do right or repent. He is unable to do anything until he has been regenerated by a sovereign arbitrary act of God. Then he repents, believes and turns to God only after he has been regenerated. That is taking the passage of Scripture "dead in sin" and making it simply ridiculous. What is meant here, of course, is that he is dead to God; the "he" in this case, is dead to God, dead to good, dead to righteousness, dead to heaven but a long way from being dead.

Some women who love pleasure are a long way from being dead. They keep the drugstores and other stores in business by the amount of extra adornment they buy. They keep the clothiers and the hat makers in business; also, they keep their husbands jumping to keep them with a new car under them and generally are a long way from dead. But they are dead in the sense the Bible meant it.

And so it is with sheep. In John 10:27, Jesus says, "My sheep hear my voice, and I know them, and they follow me." If we were to take that as meaning always that the Lord's people are sheep, then of course, we could not be men anymore; we would have to be sheep. But it is a figure of speech. So when Paul says, "Forgetting those things which are behind, and reaching forth unto those things which are before" (Phil. 3:13), he doesn't mean that we are to cease to remember all that is past and let the brushstrokes of our experience disappear like disappearing ink. If we did, we would have a blank memory and no experience at all.

## Forget About It

What did Paul forget? Paul tried to forget what kind of man he had been before. "Though I might also have confidence in the flesh. If any other man thinketh that he hath whereof he might trust in the flesh, I more: Circumcised the eighth day, of the stock of Israel, of the tribe of Benjamin, an Hebrew of the Hebrews; as touching the law, a Pharisee; concerning zeal, persecuting the church; touching the righteousness which is in the law, blameless. But what things were gain to me, those I counted loss for Christ" (Phil. 3:4-7). But he forgot these things and pressed on, not allowing any memory of yesterday to slow him down. So the proper use of remembrance is to remember the things that help us and try to forget the things that do not.

Paul forgot only those things that slowed him down and hindered him from making progress, but he said that we are to remember other things. In any time of crisis, keep in mind your past. Keep in mind your fight of affliction when you became a

Christian. Keep in mind that according to Hebrews 10:33-35, you are a gazingstock (publicly exposed to reproach). Keep in mind that you endured the spoiling of your goods (your property was plundered), and cast not away therefore your confidence, like a soldier or a group of soldiers that become suddenly frightened, lose heart, throw away their guns—the only protection they have—and make a headlong dash toward the rear. A Christian can get in that same fix.

We get the impression from some preachers that Christianity is a pink cloud upon which God floats you off to heaven without any discipline, without any will, without any purpose, without any settled confidence, but simply with a great deal of emotion we are swept along. The Bible has more to say about confidence and vows and purpose and will and determination than it does about joy. The Lord knows that a man can be happy and be a scoundrel, but the Lord also knows that if a man has set his face like a flint to do the will of God, he will not be a scoundrel but will make it through.

Satan tries to terrorize and stampede God's people. God is saying to us, "You're not green troops; don't you remember how once in your early Christian life you suffered for Christ's sake? Remember your great fight of affliction. Remember that you were made a gazingstock; people looked at you as if you were a three-headed calf in a zoo. They looked at you as if you were completely crazy. Remember that, remember the affliction you endured; remember that you became companions of people who were afflicted and persecuted, and remember that you lost your property for Christ's sake; you lost your goods for Christ's sake. Therefore, have courage and keep up your confidence."

Satan tries to terrorize, but God says, "He that shall come will come, and will not tarry" (Heb. 10:37). He will either come now to your present help if you need Him and when you need Him, or He will come to your final appearing, whichever or both. The Lord will come, so do not let it bother you. I believe in this. He will come to terminate the evil and to diadem the right.

## Live by Faith, Not by Feelings

"The just shall live by faith," not the just shall live by his feelings. Faith here is complete confidence. It is not an act of believing once done. It is not something you do and settle it. It is a complete confidence that remains with you all the time. Faith is a complete confidence. It is a state of confidence maintained—a state of confidence first in God. We must believe in God, then we must believe in His Son, Jesus Christ, in the work He did for us and the work He is now doing for us at the right hand of God. We must maintain a state of confidence in the promises of God and the certainty that God will come to our aid. A Christian is completely thrown out on God. He's thrown out on God, and the writer of the Hebrews says here that you've turned away from the world and you're attached to Jesus Christ; so be confident and maintain your confidence, for "the just shall live by his faith."

There are many times when you will not have any spiritual feeling at all; so when that time comes, live by faith. The fifteenth-century writer Thomas à Kempis said, "When the Lord withdraws his comforts from me, that is when I no longer feel like singing. When he withdraws his comforts, it is my business to remain uncomforted until which time the Lord gives me back my comforts again." So we are therefore to have our confidence, but it is a long-range confidence, not a petulant demand for immediate vindication.

Recently, books have been written on prayer that never should have been written and, unfortunately, many people buy them. They have very little discernment, and so they buy a book if it has a nice cover and they read it. Many books on prayer are dedicated to, as one man said, getting things from God. That was the name of his book, *Getting Things from God* (Charles A. Blanchard, published in 1915). God has things, and you go and get them from God.

That is one aspect of prayer, certainly, but it's only one aspect of prayer.

## Develop the Long-Range View

The eleventh chapter of Hebrews is the chapter of faith and you will find that very few of the fruits of faith were given to the people while they were on earth. They had a long-range faith that looked into the future and dared to count the things that were not as though they were, and the things that were as though they were not. They dared to believe in the long-range view, and so most of them died without seeing the fulfillment of the promises, but they lived on and died and are now with the Lord—the soul of the righteous are in the hands of God. The old apocryphal book, the Wisdom of Solomon, says this: "But the souls of the righteous are in the hand of God, and there shall no torment touch them. In the sight of the unwise they seemed to die: and their departure is taken for misery, and their going from us to be utter destruction: but they are in peace" (3:1-3).

The people of faith in the eleventh chapter of Hebrews were not the nickel-in-the-slot Christians who went to the Lord and got things from God. They believed God for things too big to get now. If you are satisfied with ten-cent jewelry, God might be willing to give it to you now; but the great things, the mighty things, God is making you wait for to discipline you.

If you want a mushroom, it will grow overnight. Let it rain and you will have a mushroom in the morning. But if you want an oak tree, wait 70 years, take the long-range view and believe for the future. I think it is entirely possible to be petulant and demanding, and go to God and say, "God, I'll have this and this and this, and I'll have that." And sometimes the Lord gives it, but see what Scripture says about that: "And he gave them their request; but sent leanness into their soul" (Ps. 106:15).

I am not saying God does not answer prayer. There are times, critical times, when God does answer prayer immediately and at once. There are times when He has to answer at once. There are times when God has to send the answer special delivery, no time to wait for the regular mail, and he does it. I have had Him do it. That is one aspect of prayer and one aspect of faith.

The other aspect is the long-range view: "The just shall live by his faith." He feels good in the morning; he will thank God and go his way. If he does not feel good in the morning, he will thank God and go his way.

I remember hearing a man testify once; I smiled at the time, but I see a lot of wisdom in what he said: "I feel just as good when I don't feel good as I do when I feel good." I believe in this kind of Christianity. God takes delight in that kind of thing. If a man only loved his wife when he felt good, and as soon as he got a headache or a pain in his chest, he did not love his wife anymore, all the homes in the world would break up overnight. But the simple fact is, love is not something that rides out on your emotions for the moment, in spite of Hollywood. Love is a fixed and settled thing. We must have a settled determination to identify ourselves with God's cause.

## A Determination to Follow Jesus

In the Old Testament, Elijah went by and flung his mantle on Elisha. Elisha caught the meaning of it and decided he was going to follow the prophet. Sometime, in getting over that fence and joining the prophet, he said to himself, "I've given up everything to follow Elijah," and he did. He turned back and said to himself, "If my cattle were alive I would be tempted to go back to my cattle; and if my plows, wooden plows, are in order I would be tempted to go back to my plows. I know what I'll do, I'll kill my cattle and use the plow for fuel and we'll have a big feast and celebrate the fact that I've quit farming and started following a prophet."

Elisha settled it, and if anybody's wife or somebody said afterward, "Elisha, do you ever think you'd go back?" Elisha said, "Go back to what? The cows are dead. Go back to what? The plows don't exist anymore; they've been burnt to ashes. There's no place to go back to." He had a settled determination that he was going to follow Christ.

I believe we ought to teach this to young Christians. We must get the idea ourselves, then teach it and show young people that when they become Christians, one aspect of their conversion is that of a settled determination to follow Jesus Christ, regardless of what it may cost or how he or she may feel about it at any given time.

A Christian's feelings are like loose change in his pocket, never the same twice. We must have a settled confidence that we are on God's side.

I had a wonderful young doctor just getting his MD visit me for two hours and 15 minutes. We discussed things pertaining to his life and psychiatrists and the anthropologists and all the rest that have greatly disturbed our young people, greatly disturbed. They say that which was right to our fathers is not right to us, and that which our fathers believed in we do not believe in anymore. "Don't you see, Mr. Tozer, that once our Christian people believed this was wrong, today they accept it?" So they make the morals to be relative. That is what you call the relativity of morals—there is nothing pinned down and nothing is right in itself. It just floats. If you think it's right, then it's right; if you do not think it's right, then it's not right. Everything floats.

A Christian knows better than that; he has settled it; he believes in God the Father Almighty. He believes in his Holy Son who died for him. He believes in the will of God as his righteousness. He believes in the Bible as the fixed revelation of divine truth.

Some of our Mennonite and Amish friends out through the state of Pennsylvania will not drive an automobile; they drive a horse and buggy. I, for my part, cannot see any morality in that; that is, I cannot see a difference between a horse and buggy and an automobile except for convenience and speed; it is just a way of getting around. I am willing to let them have their opinion about it. But that is not what you set your mind on; you set your mind to do the will of God. You can do the will of God in an airplane. I suppose you could do the will of God in a space capsule, but that is one place I don't intend to do the will of God unless He sends me; and of course, if He sends me, I will go. I doubt that He'll choose me for that.

We have to make up our minds by a long-range settled determination that we are going to bear the cross without ceasing and as far as possible without whimpering.

I read a story about a dear old Swedish woman who was dying. She was a sweet old saint and was praying to the Lord in English but with a kind of accent, and then she turned and testified, "My Father has been with me all these years and he's blessed me and kept me from sin . . . almost." She was at least honest.

It was an approximation, but she remembered a few little things that did not exactly qualify as righteousness, So she said "almost." I believe we are settled to bear the cross and do the will of God. And if there should be a necessity for a little bracket, a little "almost," then put it in there, be honest with God. But see to it that you carry the cross and live for another world than this, and serve and wait for God's time and lose whatever God calls you to lose, whatever it might be, lose it. It is all right. Lose it and honor God in everything. That is a settled determination.

God is saying to us, "I want you to call to remembrance and remember how you lived and don't get panicky and don't quit and don't get discouraged and don't give up because things aren't moving the way you think they ought to move in your life or in your church or in your home." Cast not away your confidence; the just shall live by faith. That makes me feel good just to hear Him say it. Just to know that this is the way God wants His people to live. He does not give us little wings and then say, "Fly away."

He says, "The just shall live by faith, and we walk by faith and not by sight." If any man draw back, He says, he draws back because of fear or love of this world or love of life or because of impatience. If God does not answer his prayer, he wants to get mad and quit. This is not faith. As one who believes, we are not of them that draw back; rather, we are of them that believe.

What should concern us is not how we feel but what we believe and how firm we believe it.

We look like other people, but we are not like other people; we are God's people. And when we celebrate the Lord's Supper, it is a remembrance: "This do in remembrance of me" (Luke 22:19). As we look back at all God has done, and forward to all that God will do, it ties together our yesterdays, our today and our tomorrows.

## Yesterday, Today, Forever
### by A. B. Simpson (1843–1919)

Oh how sweet the glorious message
Simple faith may claim:
Yesterday, today, forever,
Jesus is the same!
Still He loves to save the sinful,
Heal the sick and lame,
Cheer the mourner,
Still the tempest.
Glory to His name!

Yesterday, today, forever,
Jesus is the same.
All may change but Jesus never!
Glory to His name!
Glory to His name!
Glory to His name!
All may change but Jesus never!
Glory to His name!

# 15

# THE DAILY PRACTICE
# OF GOD'S PRESENCE

*These all died in faith, not having received the promises,*
*but having seen them afar off, and were persuaded of them,*
*and embraced them, and confessed that they were strangers*
*and pilgrims on the earth. For they that say such things declare plainly*
*that they seek a country. And truly, if they had been mindful of that*
*country from whence they came out, they might have had opportunity*
*to have returned. But now they desire a better country, that is, an*
*heavenly: wherefore God is not ashamed to be called their God: for he*
*hath prepared for them a city.*

HEBREWS 11:13-16

What one does occasionally does not define a person, but rather, what that individual does regularly. Anyone can do something occasionally, but most of the time that is usually accidental.

The baseball player who occasionally gets a home run but strikes out every other time is not known as a homerun king. Anybody can have a good day once in a while, but the real homerun hitters are ones who consistently hit home runs. Or, to change the illustration a little, take someone who is sick and goes to the doctor who prescribes medicine that will help him.

The instructions are that the sick man is to take the medicine regularly until it is finished. In a week, he goes back to the doctor still in the same condition that he was in the week before, with no improvement.

"Have you been taking your medicine?" the doctor asks.

"Only occasionally, when I feel like it," the man responds.

We might smile at something as silly as that, and yet there are many spiritual parallels. Our spiritual health and vitality are built upon establishing the proper spiritual disciplines and habits. People recoil at the idea of habits and consider it just routine. And yet, it is the routine that is the most productive.

Whether they acknowledge it or not, everyone has habits, but only a few carefully craft their habits in order to enhance their spiritual growth and development. How few of God's people really enjoy the fullness of their salvation! Many are satisfied with their destination, but they neglect the journey. The day-by-day experience of God's presence is something totally foreign to many Christians.

In the Old Testament, Enoch became so preoccupied with walking with God that the things of this world grew strangely dim. "He was not," the Bible says, "because God took him." I believe that once a person truly experiences the conscious, manifest presence of God, he will lose interest in everything else in this world. No longer will the cheap choruses satisfy. The flood of entertainment that has swamped the Church will leave him with a desperately empty feeling inside. And the cult of personality, which has gripped the Church these days, will no longer draw his admiration. All those things he once reveled in no longer interest him. He has discovered something far greater in God's presence.

For the serious Christian, I have a few words of encouragement. For those who are not serious, but merely curious, I have nothing really to say. But anyone who will apply simple spiritual discipline in his daily life will see a marvelous difference in his spiritual walk.

## The Discipline of Shunning the World

I do not think I can say too many times that the world is too much with us. I have often wondered why, after getting victory over the world, anybody would want to court the world and allow it back in his or her life. It must be understood most emphatically that the world around us is in conflict with the Word within us. The two are absolutely incompatible. Jesus made it plain when He said, "In the world, but . . . ." By that, He meant that although we were in the world, the world was not in us.

The evidence is all around us that it is difficult to break the tyranny of the world. Once the world gets a hold on us, it refuses to let go. And it is not hard to see this in, for example, the impulse for entertainment and fun. We certainly live in a fun generation. Unless we can have fun, and unless that thing is going to entertain us, we will wander off to something that will. I am not surprised that this is out in the world, but I am greatly disappointed that it has come into the Church.

Churches today are built upon the premise of entertainment and fun. And in some places it would be rather difficult to gain an audience unless you supplied them ample entertainment and fun. Worse than that, if there can be such a thing, is the appetite for lust and greed. Again, I do not have a hard time understanding this out in the world. But among those who have been set free by the power of God, to be driven in their personal and professional lives by lust and greed is most appalling.

The reason I stress this is that all of these are hindrances to experiencing the presence of God. They are, if I may say it this way, cheap substitutes for the real experience with God. These elements of the world dull our sense of God's presence among us.

They hinder us in several ways. The first would be in our ability to concentrate. Most people today cannot concentrate on any one thing for a significant amount of time. This is a victory for the enemy of man's soul. To occupy a man with things other than spiritual things is the predominant agenda of the devil. Unfortunately, he has the cooperation of the world around us in achieving his goal. And he does not find much resistance.

Another way of hindrance is in the area of expectation. I will mention this in more detail later on. Suffice it to say right now, the average Christian's expectation every day is in the direction of the world around him instead of expecting the Lord's presence. This I believe is a very important discipline for us, to shun the world and all its distractions. To be mindful of the danger that lurks all around us and to do something about it.

Every person needs to devise some way to discipline himself from the things of the world.

## The Discipline of Meditating on God's Word

Here is the supreme discipline for every Christian. Following our conversion to Christ, every believer has an insatiable thirst for the Word of God. Before conversion, we may have had some curiosity about the Bible and the stories of the Bible. But now, as a Christian, it is an altogether different game. The Word of

God becomes our nourishment by which we grow in the grace and knowledge of the Lord Jesus Christ.

A good deal is being said today about the art of meditation, much of it is quite dangerous. Let me just say that meditation apart from the Word of God is quite hazardous and opens us up for the delusion of the enemy. There are those who would instruct us to empty our minds (some find this rather easy) and focus within. I know what would happen to me if I tried that. I would fall fast asleep. There is nothing within anybody's soul worth meditating upon. True meditation begins with the Word of God.

I must caution here that the Bible is not an end in itself. We were not given the Bible as a substitute for God until we get to heaven. Rather, the Bible is to lead us straight into the heart and mind of God. Contemporary Christians do not seem to get this. The hymn writer Mary Ann Lathbury, in her marvelous hymn "Break Thou The Bread of Life," seems to know what this is all about. One phrase she uses explains it:

Beyond the sacred page I seek Thee, Lord;
My spirit pants for thee, O Living Word.

Some Christians read the Bible only to find some prooftext to use in their witnessing, which is more arguing that witnessing. To come to the Word for anything less than meeting God borders on sacrilege. Many come to prove a point. Some come to establish a doctrine. This, however, is quite wrong.

We must discipline ourselves to come to the Word with holy anticipation to meet with God. To come to the Bible and not be fed is the sad plight of many people today.

I would suggest we discipline ourselves to read the Bible until it comes alive—until we can almost feel the breath of God breathing upon us. David felt this way, particularly when he wrote, "As the hart panteth after the water brooks, so panteth my soul after thee, O God" (Ps. 42:1). He knew what it was to pant after God.

One dear old saint of God gave the instruction that we should nourish our soul on high thoughts of God. This can only be done through the Scriptures. As we come to the Bible, we come with the holy anticipation of actually meeting with God. Also, part of the discipline of meditating on the Scriptures is to allow the Scriptures to cleanse our thoughts and make our mind a clean sanctuary appropriate and pleasing unto the Lord.

Often while meditating upon the Scripture, a verse or a word will capture my attention. The temptation is to move on, but in disciplining myself along these lines, I have discovered that in wrestling with the Scripture the result is an experience with God.

## The Discipline of Solitude

Another discipline toward the daily practice of God's presence is the discipline of solitude. We live in a very noisy world. All around us are noises and voices that are most distracting.

Has there been a person born of woman yet unable to overcome the impulse to talk all the time? Nothing is more annoying to me when riding in an airplane than to have a young child in the seat in front of me. I can almost guarantee that during the flight the child will talk and talk and talk almost without stop.

Solitude perhaps is one of the most difficult of our spiritual disciplines. Everything in our life and the world around us mitigates against this. Because of its difficulty, this discipline is very important. What could be more important than sitting in silence before God?

Many times, when we come to God in prayer, we come with a grocery list of things we are asking for. I believe in asking God for things. I believe that it is important to come before God with a list of things that we are trusting Him for. But after all that is done, some time must be given to cultivating silence before His presence.

This takes practice and discipline, I guarantee you, and will not come easily. We must plow through all the voices around us clamoring for our attention—voices calling us away from God to do things, important things, but things nevertheless.

There is not a Christian alive but has to die, and die daily, to thoughts of self-importance. There are things that we must do, things that only we can do. Many Christians suffer from the guilt of doing nothing. Coming before God in quietness and waiting upon Him in silence can sometimes accomplish more than days and weeks of feverish activity.

David understood this very well. Under the influence of the Holy Spirit, he wrote, "Be still, and know that I am God: I will be exalted among the heathen, I will be exalted in the earth" (Ps. 46:10). It is in silence that we begin to see and then hear the pulsating heart of God. All of the nervous activity of our culture hinders us from really getting to know God as He desires to reveal Himself.

We must overcome this American mindset that says a moment of silence is a moment wasted. The discipline of silence is the price we pay to get to know God.

# The Discipline of the Daily Expectation of God's Presence

This seems to be something taken for granted, and yet I wonder: How many Christians really harbor within their own spirit the daily expectation of God's presence? How many truly expect a personal encounter with God?

It is quite important to cultivate a daily expectation of God's presence in your day. Jeremiah 29:13 admonishes us, "And ye shall seek me, and find me, when ye shall search for me with all your heart." Proverbs 8:17 states, "I love them that love me; and those that seek me early shall find me."

Let me quickly point out that this expectation must be based on the Bible and not some esoteric hope. The Christian must fearlessly repudiate anything not in harmony with the plain teaching of the Scriptures. Our daily walk is not in a vacuum; rather, it is fortified by, "Thus saith the Lord." It is the Word of the Lord that gives direction to our daily expectation of God's presence.

Each day presents a new opportunity to experience God and fellowship with Him. Nothing should so occupy the mind of the Christian than discovering God in his day. Remember, the three Hebrew children discovered God in the fiery furnace. If it was not for the fiery furnace, they never would have experienced the presence of God as they did that day. We are sometimes so anxious to get rid of the furnace and in so doing fail to experience God's presence in that unique way.

I think this is a sacred expectation for us. The mother will carry her child for nine months, and people will say of her, "She's expecting." And we all know what she is expecting. That bundle of joy that changes everything about her life from that day forward.

No less so is the expectation of God's people. My encounter with God today may be of such a nature as to alter the entire course of my life. With a sacred expectation for me to dwell upon each morning, as I get up, I look for God in all the circumstances of my day.

Let me give personal testimony that I never anticipate a day without experiencing the presence of God. Yes, some days are filled with His presence, and other days are just as barren as the desert Moses found himself in before he met God in the bush.

Start the day seeking God's presence and search for Him all through the day and revel in the gracious encounters of God throughout the day.

## The Discipline of Reverential Awe

One of the things I grieve over in the church today is that there is a lack of reverential awe or fear of God in our midst. In our worship services, a crude familiarity has developed through the years. It seems we rush in, out of breath from worldly activities, only to rush out again never having received the blessing.

I believe we need to cultivate a healthy appreciation of the holy presence of God in our midst, especially in our assemblies. There is no fear of God among us anymore. There is no holy hush that comes upon us as we supposedly sit before the living God. Our services and our singing are crude, coarse and borderline profane. All of it, in my opinion, is unbecoming of the Majesty of the glorious Christ whom we serve.

To know God is to fear Him. And this fear is to love Him as He deserves to be loved. Not the coarse, irreverent, Hollywood romantic love, but the high and holy rapturous love of the saint on fire for his Lord.

I must confess that I live each day in fear of God. It is a healthy fear. It is wonderful. It is a sense of His awe shrouding my heart and mind as I look to Him in humility.

## The Discipline of Obedience

One last discipline I need to include here is obedience. Obedience is not something that comes naturally to any of us, particularly in the spiritual realm. There are many things arrayed against us necessitating us to track all diligence in obeying the Scriptures.

There is a "once for all" factor in the Christian life. Our salvation is a once-for-all experience, but there is also the daily renewing of our walk with God. Each day we must diligently follow the leading of the Scriptures and the Word of God. One marvelous thing about the leading of the Holy Spirit is that He never leads us contrary to the clear, plain teaching of the Word of God. This cannot be stressed enough.

The key to disciplining ourselves in the area of obedience is always keeping in mind to whom we are being obedient. Of course, the resolve of my obedience is an encounter with God. The hymn writer put it this way, "Trust and obey, for there's no other way to be happy in Jesus."

The most unhappy Christians in the church today are those who are walking in disobedience. We must immediately and forthrightly discipline ourselves to obey the Word of God.

## Make Room for His Presence

To experience the presence of God is a pilgrimage of utter delight and fascination for the believer. How sad for some who live their entire lives in a way that everything can be explained. Oh, my friend, make room for mystery in your Christian life!

We are busy-beaver Christians. The average church calendar has something going on every day and night of the week. I think many things in our life and in our calendar need to go. Often we do things just because we have done them before. Or we are following the herd instinct and doing it because other people are doing it as well. Christianity, I fear, is not allergic to fads and fancies.

All of these things hinder our experiencing a conscious, manifest presence of God in our everyday life. I'm not talking about sinful things but about the things that hinder us from pressing on into His presence. What is needed today is spiritual discernment along with the courage to identify these things and root them out once and for all.

If you knew someone was coming to visit, you would cancel everything and make preparations to receive that guest. Let us make room for this guest—our Lord. And may He not be just a guest but rather an intimate companion in our day-to-day walk.

I am confident that God in His goodness will bring you to a deep experience of Himself as you seek Him with all of your heart.

# God Reveals His Presence
## by Gerhard Tersteegen (1697–1769)

God reveals His presence:
Let us now adore Him,
And with awe appear before Him.
God is in His temple:
All within keep silence,
Prostrate lie with deepest reverence. Him alone
God we own,
Him our God and Saviour:
Praise His Name for ever!

God reveals His presence:
Hear the harps resounding;
See the crowds the throne surrounding;
"Holy, holy, holy!"
Hear the hymn ascending,

Angels, saints, their voices blending.
Bow Thine ear
To us here;
Hearken, O Lord Jesus,

O Thou Fount of blessing
Purify my spirit,
Trusting only in Thy merit:
Like the holy angels
Who behold Thy glory,

May I ceaselessly adore Thee.
Let Thy will
Ever still
Rule Thy Church terrestrial,
As the hosts celestial.

---

Follow Tozer's new writings on Twitter at
http://twitter.com/tozeraw

# A.W. TOZER:
## THE AUTHORIZED BIOGRAPHY

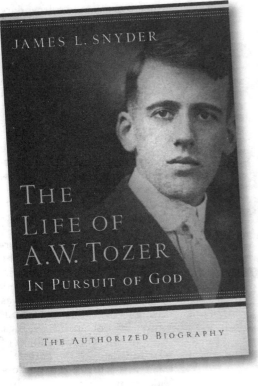

THE LIFE OF A.W. TOZER:
IN PURSUIT OF GOD
*James L. Snyder*
ISBN 978.08307.46941
ISBN 08307.46943

To understand the ministry of A.W. Tozer, it is important to know who he was, including his relationship with God. In *The Life of A.W. Tozer*, James L. Snyder lets us in on the life and times of a deep thinker who was not afraid to "tell it like it is" and never compromised his beliefs. A.W. Tozer's spiritual legacy continues today as his writings challenge readers to a deeper relationship and worship of God in reverence and adoration. Here is Tozer's life story, from boyhood to his conversion at the age of 17, to his years of pastoring and writing more than 40 books (at least two of which are regarded as Christian classics and continue to appear on bestseller lists today). Examining Tozer's life will allow you to learn from a prophet who had much to say against the compromises he observed in contemporary Christian living and the hope he found in his incredible God.

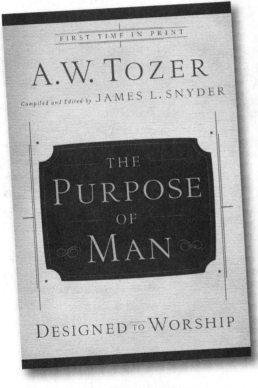

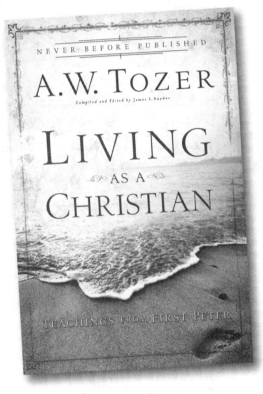